PUNCTUATION:
a programmed approach

2d edition

W. E. Perkins

North Texas State University
Denton, Texas

Published by

E47 **SOUTH-WESTERN PUBLISHING CO.**

CINCINNATI   WEST CHICAGO, ILL.   DALLAS   PELHAM MANOR, N.Y.   PALO ALTO, CALIF.

Table of Contents

To the Student

PROGRAM OBJECTIVES

If you are like most people, you realize that your punctuation skills aren't what you would like for them to be. You may not feel as confident about writing as you do about speaking because speaking doesn't require you to insert commas, semicolons, colons, periods, or other punctuation marks. This text will help you overcome some of your fears of written communication. By working with this program, you will learn to:

1. Punctuate effectively through reviewing and working with the high-frequency rules of punctuation.
2. Make applications of punctuation rules to typical business correspondence in less time and minimum effort by setting your own learning pace.
3. Assume the responsibility for your own instruction and use the skills of the teacher for diagnostic and prescribing purposes.

BEHAVIORAL OBJECTIVES

This text will help you improve your punctuation skills markedly if you will supply the needed ingredients: a strong desire to improve and a motivation to stick with the program. If you are really sincere about wanting to correct some of your punctuation deficiencies, you can. When you are finished with this learning experience, you will notice a difference in your confidence and performance levels. You will be able to:

1. Demonstrate a marked improvement in written transcripts by a one-third reduction in punctuation errors.
2. Make 25 percent fewer errors on a standard test of general punctuation ability on the posttest than on the pretest.
3. Make from 45 percent to 60 percent fewer errors in punctuating letters devoid of all marks of punctuation on the posttest than on the pretest.

INTENDED USE AND VALIDATION OF THE PROGRAM

Though not all the rules of punctuation are covered, the most common ones are embodied in the 27 rules presented in this book. The 27 basic rules account for over 98 percent of the frequency of usage in typical business correspondence.

A program can be judged only on the basis of how effective it is in changing your behavior. The question you want answered is, "What can I do after completing the programmed learning exercises that I could not do before?" The behavioral objectives will give you a very good idea of what you can expect.

The questions and responses used in this book were pilot tested and field tested. The program was reworked until it accomplished the objectives established for the program.

HOW TO PROCEED

This program will teach you the 27 basic punctuation rules. This learning may be different from anything you have experienced before because the program is designed to let you work at your own pace. After reading a unit of information called a frame, you will be instructed to respond using that information. Answers have been provided on the opposite page so that you may check the adequacy of your response immediately upon completing the frame. By reading, responding, and checking your answers, you will be able to apply the rules with complete confidence at the end of the instructional period.

In order to complete the program successfully, you should do the following:

1. Record all your responses in pencil on the programmed booklet.
2. Read each frame and respond as directed. Cover the answers on the opposite page with a sheet of paper or a 5" × 8" card. (It is very important, of course, that you do not look at the answers until <u>after</u> you have made your response.) If there are three responses to a frame, do all three before checking your answers. Be sure to keep the answers covered while you are working. After you have written your answer to the frame, move the card or sheet of paper down the page and check to see if you are right. Complete each frame in this manner.
3. You will notice that helpful information has been provided on the answer page opposite the frames. Not only is the answer given, but many times the reason <u>why</u> is also stated. Be sure to read this information as it will help you in the following frames.
4. At the end of the section, read the instructions for taking the section test. This self-check is simply a review of everything you have learned up to that point. After you have carefully reviewed all items missed on the section test, turn to the "Special Problem Areas" at the back of the text. These pages have been included to give you special reinforcement on punctuation that is most troublesome for you. If you can construct sentences of your own using the punctuation marks that you missed, you will be more apt to correct your weaknesses before moving ahead.
5. Proceed to the next section in the program and continue the reading-responding-checking process.
6. Work as rapidly as you can, but avoid hurrying. Try to comprehend the material as you go. If you should miss an item, reread the material to see if you can understand why you missed it. Review items are scattered throughout the program to reinforce a correct response every time you give one.
7. At the end of Section 7, your teacher will give you the final examination.
8. Read the discussion of the rules on the following pages before starting the program. An easy reference is provided at the end of the 27 rules for quick checking of any punctuation mark as you work through the exercises.

1. Use a *PERIOD* at the end of (a) a declarative sentence or (b) an imperative sentence.
   Ex.: Business conditions continue as usual. (Declarative)
   Ex.: Cancel all contracts with the Gray Company at once. (Imperative)

   Discussion: A declarative sentence makes a simple statement of fact, i.e., it declares something. Most sentences fall into this category. By definition, to *declare* means to make known, to reveal, to explain, or to assert. An *imperative* sentence makes a command, i.e., it tells someone to perform some type of action. Depending on the emphasis, a declarative or imperative sentence will require a period or an exclamation point.

2. Use a *PERIOD* after (a) an abbreviation which stands for a single word and (b) an abbreviation and/or initials of a proper name.
   Ex.: Charles Groton, Inc. (*Inc.* stands for incorporated.)
   Ex.: Chas. A. Groton Incorporated (*Chas.* stands for Charles; *A.* is the man's middle initial for the name Alfred.)

   Discussion: Abbreviations and initials are not difficult to recognize, but they are easy to overlook in punctuating a transcript.

3. Use a *COMMA* to set off a year date which is used to explain a preceding date of the month.
   Ex.: Operations began on May 16, 1901, at Three Rivers.

   Discussion: In the above example, 1901 defines which May 16 we are talking about. Dates may be stated in many ways, but the more parts a date contains, the more specific it becomes. NOTE:

   > the 12th (one part)
   > May 12 (two parts)
   > May 12, 1923 (three parts)
   > Wednesday, May 12, 1923 (four parts)

4. Use a *COMMA* to set off the name of a state when the name of a city precedes it.
   Ex.: We have shipped it to you in Madison, Maine, by freight collect.

   Discussion: Remember that commas surround the state when the city precedes it. Most people remember the comma between the city and state but forget the one after the state.

5. Use a *COLON* after a salutation in a business letter.
   Ex.: Dear Mrs. Colvin:

   Discussion: A colon after the salutation and a comma after the complimentary close are commonly known as *mixed* punctuation. *Open* punctuation means no punctuation at these two points. Both styles are considered correct. After a salutation, a semicolon is never appropriate; and a comma is used only in informal writing situations in which case the recipient's first name is usually stated in the salutation.

---

* The statement of the rules and examples are reprinted from Donald G. Stather, ''The Application of the Rules of Punctuation in Typical Business Correspondence'' (Doctoral Dissertation, Boston University, 1960).

6. Use a *COMMA* to follow the complimentary close of a letter.
   Ex.: Sincerely yours,

   Discussion: The complimentary close will be followed by a comma if *mixed* punctuation is used, or nothing if *open* punctuation is used. No other mark of punctuation is considered appropriate.

7. Use a *COMMA* to set off a dependent (subordinate) clause which has been transposed or placed out of order in the sentence.
   Ex.: <u>When you have shipped the order from Detroit</u>, we shall send a check.

   Discussion: A dependent clause does not express a complete thought; it adds to the meaning of the independent clause which does. When the dependent clause comes at the end of a sentence, it is said to be in its normal position. If the dependent clause introduces the sentence, it is usually followed by a comma.

8. Use a *COMMA* to separate two or more independent (coordinate) clauses when they are joined by <u>nor</u>, <u>or</u>, <u>and</u>, or <u>but</u>.
   Ex.: Your product sells itself, <u>and</u> we take pleasure in handling it.

   Discussion: Coordinate clauses are usually two equal independent clauses, each expressing a complete thought. When they are connected by the simple conjunctions (nor, or, but, and), a comma is used to separate the clauses. In other words, two separate, but related, ideas are expressed in the same sentence and are connected by a simple coordinating conjunction plus a comma. A conjunction is no more than a connector.

9. Use a *COMMA* after introductory expressions, such as *of course*, *however*, *accordingly*, *after all*, *therefore*, when they are used as conjunctions at the beginning of a sentence, in order to make a distinction between the thought that precedes and the thought that follows the expression.
   Ex.: <u>Accordingly</u>, your request has been handled by another office.

   Discussion: Sometimes a sentence will begin with a connector which joins the sentence with the preceding thought. These connectors are called longer coordinating conjunctions. They are to be distinguished from the simple coordinating conjunctions discussed in Rule 8 above. A sentence will frequently begin with a longer coordinating conjunction, but rarely will it begin with a simple coordinating conjunction. Both types, however, connect one thought with another because they are conjunctions.

10. Use a *COMMA* to set off a parenthetical expression (word, phrase, or clause) when the degree of separation is not great enough to require the use of parentheses or dashes.
    Ex.: We appreciate the remittance, <u>small as it is</u>, received today.

    Discussion: The word *parenthetical* derives from the word *parenthesis*. A parenthetical is an additional word, clause, etc., placed as an explanation or comment within an already complete sentence. Such thoughts are generally considered as interruptors and are somehow separated from the rest of the sentence. Minor parentheticals are set off with commas instead of parentheses. In either case, strong or minor, the interrupting idea can be removed without changing the completeness of the sentence.

11. Use a *HYPHEN* when two or more words have the force of a single modifier before a noun.
    Ex.: It is a well-known fact that our product reaches the far corners of the earth.

    Discussion: Such modifiers are called compound adjectives. A *compound adjective* simply means that the modifying adjective consists of two or more words but is meant to be read as one word. Only compound adjectives that precede the noun they modify are hyphenated. Those following the noun are not joined together into a single unit.

12. Use a *COMMA* to set off a nonrestrictive clause or phrase.
    Ex.: Your salespeople, whom I met yesterday, are outstanding.

    Discussion: A *restrictive clause* is essential to the complete meaning of the sentence; a *nonrestrictive clause* is nonessential. According to the discussion in Rule 10, we know that nonessential material is occasionally separated from the remainder of the sentence by commas. If the material is restricted (essential) for complete meaning, no commas are used. Punctuation is required around the nonessential material if it is not needed to identify the noun that the phrase modifies.

13. Use an *APOSTROPHE* to show singular or plural possessive.
    Ex.: Each clerk's duty is obvious. (Singular possessive)
    Ex.: Our customers' satisfaction is the key to our continued success. (Plural possessive)

    Discussion: An *apostrophe* is used to show the possessive form of nouns. As a general rule, singular possessive (SP) requires an 's, whereas plural possessive (PP) requires an s'. There are exceptions, of course, such as in cases where the plural form of the word is different from the singular form. (Ex.: man→men) Unless there is no change in the word form, a discrimination must be made between SP and PP by the placement of the apostrophe. Again, since most plurals are formed by adding s, distinctions are as follows:

Singular	Plural	Singular Possessive	Plural Possessive
mule	mules	mule's	mules'

14. Use a *PERIOD* to separate (a) a whole number from a decimal fraction and (b) dollars from cents.
    Ex.: This constitutes 24.5 percent of our income. (Decimal fraction)
    Ex.: We have paid $459.50 in taxes during the current year. (Dollars and cents)

    Discussion: Omitting the period in these decimals is a rare punctuation error. Since figures constitute a high portion of business writing, one should remember that no space follows the decimal.

15. Use a *COMMA* to set off words or phrases which explain a preceding noun (appositives).
    Ex.: To Lynn Blake, our sales manager, goes much of the credit.

    Discussion: An *appositive* renames the noun it modifies. Literally, an *appositive* is a word or expression beside another so that the second explains and has the same grammatical construction as the first. Appositives may be either essential or nonessential. If the word or phrase is needed to identify the noun (essential), no commas can be used. If the phrase merely describes or renames the noun (nonessential), commas are used.

16. Use a *COMMA* after (a) each element except the last or (b) each pair of elements except the last in a <u>series</u> of coordinating nouns, adjectives, verbs, or adverbs.
    Ex.: Not long ago, we sold only <u>groceries</u>, <u>clothes</u>, and <u>hardware</u> in our store. (Noun series)
    Ex.: These scatter rugs are available in <u>green and white</u>, <u>blue and white</u>, and <u>green and gray</u> during the sale. (Pairs of adjectives series)

Discussion: A *series* is a group or number of similar or related things arranged in sequence. When this group of things consists of three or more items, commas are used to connect the separate parts. <u>No comma is necessary after the last item in the series.</u>

17. Use a *COMMA* to set off titles and degrees following a person's name.
    Ex.: Mail all educational literature to <u>Donna Grayson**,** principal</u>, beginning May 10. (Principal is a title.)

Discussion: A title following a person's name is punctuated with commas, but a title preceding a name requires no punctuation. When the title follows, it is considered a nonessential appositive; when a title precedes, it is considered essential.

18. Use a *COMMA* to set off *Inc.* and *Ltd.* following the name of a company.
    Ex.: Thacker & Company, Ltd., will supply your catalogue.

Discussion: Although these abbreviations are usually treated as nonessential appositives, no commas are used to separate the full words *company, corporation,* or *incorporated* from the preceding company name.

19. Use a *PERIOD* at the end of a sentence embodying a courteous request in the form of a question.
    Ex.: May we have your reply to the letter as soon as possible<u>.</u>

Discussion: In business writing we frequently request some kind of action. Although this may take an interrogative form, we don't really expect to receive a direct answer to the question. Instead we want to see the action being requested. These statements are commonly referred to as *polite requests*. In the above example, you don't really want the reader to say, "Yes, you may have my reply as soon as possible." Rather, you want the person to write back as soon as possible taking the <u>action</u> politely requested.

20. Use a *COLON* following expressions which contain words such as *thus*, *that is*, or *as follows* used to introduce enumerations, tabulations, or long quotations.
    Ex.: You are requested to bring the following items to the conference<u>:</u> sales records, manuals, calculators, scratch pads, pencils, and several good ideas for sales promotions.

Discussion: A colon represents a strong break (pause) in continuity and indicates that something major is about to follow. An *enumeration* is a list of items; a *tabulation* is an orderly arrangement of items; and a *quotation* is the cited words of an authority. Normally a lead-in phrase will introduce the colon. A complete sentence will always precede a colon; and one will frequently follow a colon, such as in a long, formal quote.

21. Use an *APOSTROPHE* to indicate contractions of words.
    Ex.: We <u>can't</u> be certain of profits unless we all cooperate.

Discussion: A contraction is the shortening of a word or phrase by the omission of one or more letters. An apostrophe is substituted at the point where the letters have been omitted.

22. Use *QUOTATION MARKS* to set off (a) words or phrases that are intended to be emphasized; (b) slang or coined words or phrases which might cheapen the text if it were not known that the writer is aware of them; (c) a word or phrase intended to be awkward, whimsical, or humorous; (d) a word or phrase if the expression *so-called* can be mentally supplied before it; or (e) a technical trade name.
Ex.: If you can produce some "extra" orders this month . . .
Ex.: If it can be "plasticated," Plastics, Inc., will do it.
Ex.: Ed Barrow is the "smilingest" person on our staff.
Ex.: We expect to deliver the "knockout punch" at the meeting.
Ex.: Without a doubt, "Multibestos" is the answer to your brake problems.

Discussion: The most common use of quotation marks, of course, is to introduce a direct quotation. Quotation marks may also be used at the discretion of the writer to set off or to call attention to a word or phrase.

23. Use a *COMMA* to set off digits in groups where numbers consist of four or more digits (except in series numbers).
Ex.: Nearly 49,000 free packets have been sent out this year.

Discussion: Large numbers over three digits are difficult to read. For this reason the writer facilitates the reading by dividing a figure at the thousands, millions, billions, and trillions digits.

24. Use a *SEMICOLON* to separate the independent clauses of a compound sentence when either one or both clauses are punctuated by one or more commas.
Ex.: Twenty-five years ago, during a period of great prosperity, our business was incorporated; and today we are looking optimistically toward a very prosperous future.

Discussion: In Rule 8 the point was made that a comma is used to separate two independent clauses connected by one of the simple coordinating conjunctions. Rule 24 is merely an extension of Rule 8. When either of the clauses already contains a comma, the break at the conjunction needs to be stronger. The semicolon is stronger than a comma.

25. Use a *QUESTION MARK* after a direct question.
Ex.: What is the reason for the delay in shipping our order?

Discussion: When the intent of the interrogator is to obtain a direct answer, a question mark is used to punctuate the sentence. A question is an inquiry through which the asker seeks answers to problems about which data is lacking. A direct question requires a direct response.

26. Use a *COLON* to separate hours and minutes in indicating time.
Ex.: All employees are expected to be at their desks by 9:05 a.m.

Discussion: Time is frequently expressed in figures. The figure(s) to the left of the colon represents hours; the figures to the right of the colon represent minutes past the hour.

27. Use a *SEMICOLON* to separate independent clauses closely connected in meaning and not joined by a conjunction.
    Ex.: You have requested our cooperation; we have complied.

Discussion: Again, in Rule 8 it was stated that two related ideas expressed in the same sentence are separated by a comma when a simple coordinating conjunction joins the two thoughts. Rule 27 states that whenever the simple conjunction is left out, a stronger break than a comma is needed. The semicolon serves the purpose of connecting the two related ideas. In most cases where the conjunction is missing, a period would serve just as well, except that the writer tries to avoid short, choppy sentences.

Easy Reference for Punctuation Rules

	Rule No.	Use
APOSTROPHE	13	Singular or plural possessives
	21	Contractions
COLON	5	Salutations
	20	After *thus*, *that is*, and *as follows* indicating a strong break
	26	Time (hours and minutes)
COMMA	3	Date, month, and year
	4	City, state
	6	Complimentary close
	7	Dependent clauses
	8	Independent clauses
	9	Introductory expressions
	10	Parenthetical expressions
	12	Nonrestrictive clauses or phrases
	15	Appositives
	16	Series
	17	Titles and degrees
	18	Set off *Inc.* and *Ltd.*
	23	Numbers of four or more digits
HYPHEN	11	Compound adjectives
PERIOD	1	Declarative and imperative sentences
	2	Abbreviations
	14	Whole numbers from decimal fractions and dollars from cents
	19	Courteous requests in question form
QUESTION MARK	25	Direct questions
QUOTATION MARKS	22	Words and phrases used for emphasis or slang and for words and phrases which are awkward, whimsical, humorous, etc.
SEMICOLON	24	Independent clauses with internal punctuation
	27	Related independent clauses

Learning is the result of the right kind of practice.

SECTION 1

Application Summary:

. . . **Period** after a declarative sentence
. . . **Exclamation point** after an interjection
. . . **Question mark** after a direct question
. . . **Period** after an abbreviation or an initial
. . . **Period** separating a whole number and a decimal fraction
. . . **Period** after a polite request

1

(A) (This sentence contains a subject and a verb and expresses a complete thought.)
B (The verb is missing.)
(C) (*You* is the understood subject.)

2

fact
command

3

(B) and (C)

4

A. you.
B. fared.

5

A. No punctuation is required. (This is not a complete sentence.)
B. you.

6

. or ! (Either is acceptable.)

The minimum requirements for a sentence are that it contain a subject and a verb and express a complete thought.

Circle the letters of the examples below that are complete sentences:

    A. *All of us are consumers since we buy and use goods and services*
    B. *About two-thirds of the world's population*
    C. *Please close the door*

1

Use a period at the end of a sentence that states a fact or gives a command.

    Ex.: 1. The secretary was late for work.
          2. Get me the *Gomez* dossier from the file.

Example 1 is a statement of _____.
Example 2 is a _____.

2

A statement of fact is commonly called a declarative sentence because it declares or <u>states</u> something. An imperative sentence requests or <u>commands</u> someone to do something.

Circle the letters of the following sentences that are declarative:

    A. *Pay your bill promptly when it comes due.*
    B. *An economic system is simply an arrangement for satisfying human wants.*
    C. *Business supplies us with goods, services, and jobs.*

3

A period is used at the end of both a declarative and an imperative sentence.

Punctuate the examples in Frames 4 and 5 that are complete sentences:

    A. *Economics is also concerned with helping you choose from and use wisely the many things offered to you_*
    B. *Maria, budget your spending money this month and tell me next month how you fared_*

4

    A. *Until you have paid this month's charges_*
    B. *Your local broker can describe over-the-counter stocks to you_*

5

A declarative or imperative sentence can be emotional or emphatic. In this case you may want to use an <u>exclamation point</u>. Only the writer knows what emphasis is intended.

Punctuate the following sentence as you interpret the emphasis:

    *Natural and capital resources would be of little value without people to work_*

6

7

Whew**!** call**!** (An interjection is something that is thrown in without grammatical connection. It is not a sentence, but an exclamation point is used to show surprise or excitement.)

8

A. Either a **.** or an **!** is correct depending upon your own particular emphasis.
B. Probably a **.** is sufficient. (Be careful not to overuse the exclamation. Save it so that when you really want to emphasize something you can.)

9

A. Wow**!** Bertram's**!** sale**!** (Excitement is probably shown by these short statements.)
B. You are absolutely correct! This is not a complete sentence and should not be punctuated. (See Frame 1 if you missed it.)
C. lose**.** (or **!**) (Again, you have to decide the emphasis.)

10

direct
indirect

11

Ⓐ

12

Ⓑ

13

A. Bradstreet**?** (A direct question)
B. deadline**.** (An indirect question)

4

An exclamation at the beginning of a sentence will be punctuated with an exclamation point even though the interjection may not be a complete sentence.

Punctuate the following example:

*Whew_ That was certainly a close call_*

7

Punctuate the examples in Frames 8 and 9 with a period or an exclamation point:

A. *The stock market in 1929 crashed with a force that shook the world for several years to follow_*
B. *A society pays for the cost of crime several times_*

8

A. *Wow_ Hurry to Bertram's_ You won't believe their fantastic sale_*
B. *Which is certainly priced right_*
C. *Leave the speculative stocks alone unless you have money that you can afford to lose_*

9

Use a question mark after a direct question that requires an answer, but <u>not</u> after an indirect question that requires no answer. A period usually follows an indirect question.

Ex.: 1. What should be the role of the federal government in business affairs?
     2. I wonder if the average citizen has a healthy attitude toward taxes.

In the above examples Sentence 1 asks a(n) _____ question;
Sentence 2 asks a(n) _____ question.

10

Circle the letters of the examples in Frames 11 and 12 that are direct questions:

A. *Do you know if you are going to join the credit union this fall or not*
B. *I have been asked if I am going to join the credit union this fall*

11

A. *Larry wanted to know who is responsible for determining fiscal policy*
B. *Who is responsible for determining fiscal policy*

12

Punctuate the examples in Frames 13 and 14:

A. *What is meant by a rating in Dun and Bradstreet_*
B. *Lyle was asked if he would kindly write the Department of Internal Revenue before the April 15 tax deadline_*

13

14

A. products. (A statement that is an indirect question)
B. being? (A direct question)
C. This is not a complete sentence and should not be punctuated.

15

medical doctor
mister
junior
miss (*Miss* is not an abbreviation and therefore requires no period.)

16

A. The H. M. Madsen Co. of Washington, DC, is transferring its operations.

B. Capt. Sally G. Caruthers of Lincoln, NE 68501-5244
(NOTE: No periods nor extra space are used in a two-letter state abbreviation. Place the state abbreviation in all capitals and space twice before the ZIP Code.)

17

A. T. C. Lamas and L. H. Harrison were honored at the June banquet.
B. The engine of the car reached 60 r.p.m. at 95 m.p.h.

18

*A space is optional wherever an asterisk is shown below.

At exactly 2 P. M. a representative of the Dept. of H.*E.*W. left the U.*S.*A. for Bolivia.

19

No. (The period after the abbreviation also serves as the period for the end of the sentence.)

A. I have always wondered how prices are set on certain products_
B. When did the Federal Reserve system come into being_
C. Today approximately one out of six_

14

Use a period after an abbreviation or an initial. The period indicates that part of the word has been left out.

Ex.: 1. Michi O. Masami, M.D.
2. Mr. William Smith, Jr.
3. Miss Lillian Jarnagin

M.D. stands for _____ .
Mr. stands for _____ .
Jr. stands for _____ .
Miss stands for _____ .

15

A space normally follows an abbreviation. However, if the abbreviation is not a capital letter, no space is necessary.

Ex.: 1. Dr. I. Clendenon will not be in until 9:30 A. M. this week.
2. A good typist will easily type 65 net w.p.m. in 5 minutes.

Insert periods and indicate the proper spacing in the following sentences: (Draw an arrow where a space is needed.)

A. The H_M_ Madsen Co_ of Washington, DC, is transferring its operations.
B. Capt_ Sally G_ Caruthers of Lincoln, NE_   68501-5244

16

Draw an arrow to the points that need a space following the abbreviations:

A. T.C. Lamas and L.H. Harrison were honored at the June banquet.
B. The engine of the car reached 60 r.p.m. at 95 m.p.h.

17

When three or more abbreviations occur together (consecutively), the space following the period is optional.

Punctuate and indicate by an arrow where a space must follow the abbreviation:

At exactly 2 P_M_ a representative of the Dept_ of H_E_W_ left the U_S_A_ for Bolivia.

18

If an abbreviation occurs at the end of a sentence, do not use two periods together.

Is this sentence correct? _____ .
(Yes/No)

Stop by the office tomorrow at 2:15 p.m..

19

20

A. E_ Inc_., Mass_. (Since *Miss* is not an abbreviation, no period is used following this title. Only <u>one</u> period is necessary to end a sentence, even when the sentence ends with an abbreviation.)
B. etc_. **?** (Do you see that Sentence B is a direct question?)

21

Yes. (The abbreviation stands for United Nations Educational, Scientific, and Cultural Organization.)

22

Ⓐ

23

The asterisk (*) means that the periods after each abbreviation are optional.

A. a_.m_. Ltd_., No_. 4154_.
B. R_. Blvd_. Mich_., N_.*A_.*T_.*O_. secretary_.

24

A. Ms_. E_. St_. Louis vs_. game**?**
B. Ouch**!** Corp_., Inc_., today_. (or **!**)

8

Question marks, exclamation points, or commas may follow a period in an abbreviation.

Ex.: 1. Was Julius Caesar killed in 44 B.C. or A.D.?
2. Ronnie Kline at age 21 had completed a Ph.D.!

Insert the correct punctuation at the points indicated:

A. *Miss_ E_ Aponte purchased 100 shares of preferred stock in Woodbury, Inc_, of Lowell, Mass_ _*
B. *Should housing be based on the individual family, e.g., its needs, desires, financial ability, etc_ _*

20

Many organizations omit periods after abbreviations of their names. This practice is at the option of the particular organization.

Ex.: 1. **The YMCA has served communities faithfully for many years.**
2. **UBC, United Bank of California, serves UCLA, USC, and all of Los Angeles.**

Such abbreviations may usually be written either way—periods or no periods. Both are acceptable, but it is <u>best</u> to write the name the way the organization writes it.

Could this abbreviation be correct with periods? UNESCO _____
(Yes/No)

21

When writing an abbreviated name, such as SEATO or CTA, you can omit the periods after each abbreviation if: (Circle the letter of the correct answer.)

A. *the organization writes its own name without the periods.*
B. *you feel like omitting the periods.*
C. *the English teacher says it is incorrect to use the periods.*
D. *you are writing instead of typing.*

22

Punctuate the sentences in Frames 23 and 24 by inserting the necessary question marks, periods, and exclamation points: (Watch for periods after abbreviations, especially those followed by commas.)

A. *At 9 am sharp the management of Crowder and Banes, Ltd, called an emergency meeting to discuss Procedure No 4154*
B. *Miss R Lance, who lives on Granger Blvd in Grand Rapids, Mich, received a phone call last week from the NATO secretary*

23

A. *Was Ms Martha Baldwin of E St Louis at the Cardinals vs the Braves baseball game*
B. *Ouch Chrysler Corp, Basic, Inc, and General Motors all dropped two points on the stock exchange today*

24

25

decimal fraction
dollars from cents

26

A. 1.6   4.8
B. $81.50 $96.33

(Notice that there is no period at the end of a phrase.)

27

($25)

28

Ⓐ Ⓒ and Ⓓ are redundant.
B is correct. Remember, the decimal and zeroes are unnecessary in even amounts of money, unless the sentence contains both even and uneven amounts. In this case you would use zeroes for consistency in stating the figures.

29

$19.95 $12.50

Use a period to separate whole numbers from decimal fractions and dollars from cents.

> Ex.: 1. The federal government owns 763.0 million acres of land in the U.S.
> 2. Emile borrowed $10.50 from me.

In Example 1 a period is used in the figure 763.0 to distinguish the whole number from the _____.
In Example 2 a period is inserted in the amount $10.50 to separate _____ *from* _____.

25

No space is necessary after the period in decimal fractions nor in dollars and cents.

> Ex.: 1.4 of $3.75   <u>not</u>   1. 4 of $3. 75

Write correctly in the blanks of each of the phrases below the amounts indicated in parentheses:

> A. *When converting miles into kilometers, multiply the number of miles by* _____ *(one decimal six); three miles equals* _____ *(four decimal eight) kilometers.*
> B. *A premium for $5,000 of straight life insurance at age 25 ranging from* _____ *(eighty-one dollars and fifty cents) to* _____ *(ninety-six dollars and thirty-three cents)*

26

Money in <u>even</u> amounts is preferably written with no decimal point or zeroes. The decimal and zeroes are redundant (unnecessary).

> Ex.: 1. $47   not $47.00   nor $47.
> 2. $6   not $6.00   nor $6.

Circle the correct answer below:

> *We gave ($25./$25/$25.00) to the Cancer Society.*

27

Which of these sentences contain redundant parts? (Circle the letter of the correct answer(s).)

> A. *Send only $3.00 in box tops.*
> B. *That company's stock is now $368 a share.*
> C. *The cost of her new car was $11,680.00.*
> D. *To find out the current value of $1. in England, I will look in the newspaper for the foreign exchange rate for pounds.*

28

Punctuate the following sentence according to the information given in parentheses:

> *During our summer sale, hand mixers that once sold for 1995 (nineteen dollars and ninety-five cents) are now 1250 (twelve dollars and fifty cents).*

29

30

Ⓑ (In Sentence A the period is used to end the sentence, not as a decimal.)

31

A. 0.3   0.9
B. 17.75 yds.   15.98 m.

32

Action (You are expecting them to reply, not to write back and say, "Yes, you may have my quick reply.")

33

does not

34

Ⓐ (Sentence B is a question, not a request, and expects a direct answer.)

35

Ⓒ

36

question
does
question mark
(NOTE: This statement definitely expects to be answered.)

Circle the letter of the sentence that contains a redundant part:

   A. *We decided that the old car was worth $300.*
   B. *That pile of junk isn't worth $20.!*

30

Punctuate the following sentences:

   A. *To convert feet into meters, multiply by 03 (zero decimal three); for yards, multiply by 09 (zero decimal nine).*
   B. *That company converted our order for 1775 (seventeen decimal seventy-five) yds of wire to the metric equivalent, 1598 (fifteen decimal ninety-eight) m*

31

Use a period after a polite request which is stated in question form but which calls for action rather than an answer.

   Wrong: Could I have your reply to this letter as soon as possible?
   Right: May I have your quick reply to this letter.

Do the above examples call for action or for an answer to the question? _____
                                                       (Action/Answer)

32

Some statements, although in question form, expect no direct answer. Such statements request the person to take action (do something) rather than to answer the question directly. These statements are called *polite requests*.

   A polite request (does/does not) expect a direct answer.

33

Which of these sentences is a polite request? (Circle the letter of the correct answer.)

   A. *Would you please let me know your decision soon_*
   B. *Will your decision be difficult to make_*

34

Even though a statement may appear to be a question, it will take a period at the end if the sentence is: (Circle the letter of the correct answer.)

   A. *stated in question form.*
   B. *long and complex.*
   C. *a request expecting action rather than words.*

35

Was my name selected as one of the grand winners

   The above statement is a (question/polite request) because it (does/does not) ask a direct question requiring an answer. The end punctuation mark should be a (period/question mark).

36

37

Yes.
A period

38

questions

39

Yes. (The request expects action rather than a direct answer; you want the person to actually send the applicant rather than answer, "Yes, I will send the applicant over.")

40

Yes.
No.
polite request

41

A. **?** Q (Although you may not expect the person to answer, "Yes, I sometimes wonder," the sentence is not a request.)

B. **.** PR (The sentence is a request and does not expect the person to actually give you permission to congratulate the individual.)

42

A. **.** PR (The statement is a polite request—a suggestion calling for action rather than a direct answer.)

B. **?** Q (This sentence expects a direct yes or no answer.)

*May I take this opportunity to thank you for your excellent service_*

To find the correct end punctuation for the above sentence, you must ask yourself the following questions:

1. Is the sentence a request (a suggestion)?
2. If it is, then ask the following question: Does it require a <u>direct answer</u>? (If it does require a direct answer, then the end punctuation must be a question mark. If it does not require a direct answer, then the sentence is a <u>polite request</u> and must be punctuated with a period.)

Is the first sentence in this frame a polite request? _____
What mark of punctuation is required? _____

37

A statement may not require a direct answer but can still be a question rather than a polite request.

Ex.: 1. What is the definition of the word *intestate*?
   2. Isn't the word *interstate* completely different from the word *intestate*?

Even though a direct answer may not be expected, these examples are _____.

38

Would you please send the applicant over to my office tomorrow

Is this a polite request? _____ *(Yes/No) Why?* _____
_____

39

Won't you please look over the enclosed booklet and let us know your reaction?

A. Is the above statement a request? _____
B. Does it expect a direct answer? _____
C. Therefore, the sentence is a _____.
        (polite request/direct question)

40

Place a period or a question mark at the end of each sentence in Frames 41 and 42. Then mark the sentence <u>Q</u> for question or <u>PR</u> for polite request.

*A. Don't you sometimes wonder why you ever got up in the morning_* _____
*B. May I congratulate you on your recent success_* _____

41

---

*A. Why not bring your bills to us and let us consolidate your debts_* _____
*B. Did you like the suggestion_* _____

42

15

43

ⓒ (The sentence is an indirect question. It is first of all not a request; second, it is not stated in question form.)

44

request
question
action
answer

45

a question mark
an exclamation point
a period

46

a period

47

A. Hurry! $3,00   budget?.
B. U.S.   2.2   .99 kilograms.

48

A. H. Raines, Inc., $846.50   Mr.   Jr.,   H.S.?
B. Fri.   10 A. M.
C. Dr. Kato   1.2 hours.

I have written you several times asking if you will please pay your overdue account

The above sentence is: (Circle the letter of the correct answer.)

    A. *a polite request.*
    B. *a direct question.*
    C. *an indirect question.*

43

The requirements of a polite request are that the statement indeed be a _____ and the request be stated in _____ form. Most of the time the request will call for _____ rather than words and will not require a direct _____ .

44

Fill in the blanks in Frames 45 and 46 from the following selection: a question mark, a period, and an exclamation point.

    A direct question requires _____ .
    An emphatic statement of emotion takes _____ .
    An indirect question normally will be punctuated by _____ .

45

    A polite request is punctuated with _____ .

46

Make the necessary changes, deletions, and insertions in punctuation in the sentences in Frames 47 and 48:

    A. *Hurry Won't you let us show you how you can save from $3.00 to $5 on your weekly food budget?*
    B. *US units of 22 (two decimal two) pounds equal 99 (decimal ninety-nine) kilograms*

47

    A. *Would it be possible for H Raines, Inc, to raise $84650 (eight hundred forty-six dollars and fifty cents) for Mr Todd Chandler, Jr, a senior at Margulies H.S.*
    B. *All students must attend the conference Fri morning at 10 AM*
    C. *We are asking if all would please give Dr Kato their undivided attention for just 12 (one decimal two) hours*

48

You have just completed the first section of this program. Turn to the next page and read the directions for taking the section test. Please keep in mind that in this first test your concern will be with periods, exclamation points, and question marks. Disregard commas for now.

DIRECTIONS FOR THE SECTION TESTS

1. Do not worry about commas, semicolons, etc. Your concern in this section is the use of the period, question mark, and exclamation point. Please note that the letters used in the section tests are not good business letters—they are extremely over-punctuated. The intent is to make you overlearn. If you can pass the section tests, you should have no trouble with the final examination.

2. Read the letter carefully inserting, changing, and deleting punctuation as necessary. Please use a pencil so that you may change marks easily.

3. The (E) in the letter stands for the end of a sentence. You are to insert the proper end punctuation at these points. The information in parentheses indicates the decimal fraction or the amount of money.

4. When you are finished, proofread your letter again and insert additional punctuation if necessary, until you are certain all punctuation is correct.

5. After you have finished the letter, tear out the next page, which gives the letter as it should be punctuated. Circle all punctuation marks in your letter that differ from the key. The next step is a very important one.

6. Once your errors have been circled, find the numbers you missed on the **REVIEW SHEET** and read the number of the frame where that particular rule is discussed in the programmed booklet. Be sure to go back and look up the suggested frame for every item missed before continuing to the next section. In this way you will profit from your mistakes, and misunderstandings will be cleared up immediately. When you review, you may want to ask the teacher to explain things to you that you just can't seem to straighten out on your own. Your teacher will be glad to provide this remedial attention when you show a sincere interest in learning.

October 13, 19—

Miss Shirley E Will
36497 Mt St Mary's Road
Anderson, IN   46011-1044

Dear Miss Will:

SUBJECT: Chemical No 439244

The R T Frantz Co has indicated to us that you wish to purchase 47 (four decimal seven) lbs of Chemical No 439244, which sells for $1635 (sixteen dollars and thirty-five cents) a pound (E) Our representative, J M Trammel, Jr, would be pleased to discuss this order with you (E) Are you familiar with our new public relations agent (E)

Dr Trammel is a biologist from UCLA and can show you why Ramar Products, Inc, is your best bet if you are looking for an effective gas that can rid your store of pests for less than $80 (eighty dollars) (E) Give him a call around 1 pm any day this week (E) He will be glad to stop by your office at 9035 (nine hundred three decimal five) Bryce Canyon Ave for a free demonstration (E) You are still located on Bryce, aren't you (E) Do you know for sure that 47 (four decimal seven) lbs is the exact amount you will require (E) This particular chemical has been drastically increased in potency, you know (E) Ask anyone who has used it recently (E)

At any rate, won't you give Dr Trammel a call (E) His assistant, Ying Shen, will set up an appointment for you at your convenience (E) Could I suggest that the three of us get together for lunch sometime soon after you have had your initial meeting (E)

Sincerely yours,

Mrs Cynthia Howell

grc

October 13, 19—

Miss[1] Shirley E[2] Will
36497 Mt[3] St[4] Mary's Road
Anderson, IN   46011-1044

Dear Miss Will:

SUBJECT: Chemical No[5] 439244

The R[6] T[7] Frantz Co[8] has indicated to us that you wish to purchase 4[9]7 lbs[10] of Chemical No[11] 439244, which sells for $16[12] 35 a pound[13] Our representative, J[14] M[15] Trammel, Jr[16], would be pleased to discuss this order with you[17] Are you familiar with our new public relations agent?[18]

Dr[19] Trammel is a biologist from UCLA[20] and can show you why Ramar Products, Inc[21], is your best bet if you are looking for an effective gas that can rid your store of pests for less than $80[22] [23] Give him a call around 1 p[24] m. any day this week[25] He will be glad to stop by your office at 903[26]5 Bryce Canyon Ave[27] for a free demonstration[28] You are still located on Bryce, aren't you?[29] Do you know for sure that 4[30]7 lbs[31] is the exact amount you will require?[32] This particular chemical has been drastically increased in potency, you know[33] Ask anyone who has used it recently[34]

At any rate, won't you give Dr[35] Trammel a call[36] His assistant, Ying Shen, will set up an appointment for you at your convenience[37] Could I suggest that the three of us get together for lunch sometime soon after you have had your initial meeting[38]

Sincerely yours,

Mrs[39] Cynthia Howell

grc

SECTION 1
REVIEW SHEET

If you missed no.	See Frame no.	If you missed no.	See Frame no.
1	15	26	25
2	15	27	15
3	15	28	2
4	15	29	10
5	15	30	25
6	15	31	15
7	15	32	10
8	15	33	2
9	25	34	2
10	15	35	15
11	15	36	32 & 33
12	25	37	2
13	2	38	32 & 33
14	15	39	15
15	15		
16	15		
17	2		
18	10		
19	15		
20	21 & 22		
21	15		
22	27		
23	2		
24	15 & 16		
25	2		

Please turn to page 208 to record Section 1 test errors and to restudy any punctuation rules with which you are still having difficulty.

Learning can be a chore or a natural process, depending upon perception of the task.

SECTION 2

Application Summary

. . .   **Comma** in a number of four digits or more
. . .   **Commas** in a series of coordinating nouns, adjectives,
         verbs, or adverbs
. . .   **Commas** around the word *etc.*
. . .   **Commas** in a date
. . .   **Commas** after the city and the state
. . .   **Commas** setting off a person's title or degree
. . .   **Commas** around the words *Inc.* and *Ltd.*
. . .   **Comma** after a complimentary close
. . .   **Colon** after a salutation

49

Ⓑ   (Sentence A is incorrect because the four-digit figure should be written $1,000.)

NOTE: No space follows the comma used to punctuate a figure.

50

$43,672   1,642,791 $9,989.49   1,497.9

51   four
comma

52   (49275)   (3872)   491   (6989)   ($4394.52)

487.2   27.3   324.8   .073   869.4326

53

A. 48,932 people
B. None

54

No. (Usually only amounts or quantities require commas.)

If a number has four or more digits, it probably cannot be read with ease. Therefore, use a comma in numbers of four or more digits.

Wrong:	4067	62398	1924093
Right:	4,067	62,398	1,924,093

Is A or B punctuated correctly? (Circle the letter of the correct answer.)

A. *The interest on $1000 for a 60-day loan at 9 percent is $15.*
B. *During the stock market boom of the "roaring twenties," a buyer of $10,000 worth of stocks had to put up only $2,500 or less in cash and simply borrow the difference, pledging the newly bought stocks as collateral.*

49

Numbers are set off from the decimal point by threes. To punctuate figures of four or more digits, count from the decimal point or from the far right digit of the number. Now insert a comma where appropriate in each of the following numbers:

$43672   *1642791*   *$9989.49*   *1497.9*

50

Most numbers of _____ or more digits should be punctuated with a _____ so that they may be read easily.

51

Circle the numbers that require commas:

49275	*3872*	*491*	*6989*	*$4394.52*
487.2	*27.3*	*324.8*	*.073*	*869.4326*

52

Of course, certain numbers should not be punctuated even if they are four digits or more.

Year:	By 1990
Address:	48737 N. Jackson Street
ZIP Code:	Nashville, TN 37202-5691

How would you punctuate the following numbers?

A. *48932 people*
B. *3296 S. Beale Avenue*

53

Other kinds of numbers that should not be punctuated are those that are meant to be read as one whole unit.

Ex.: 1. The car's serial #4927406
      2. My driver's license number S581586
      3. Your Policy No. 94387614

Would this long number need commas? Account No. 4927498

54

55

    A. $40,000
    B. $400,000

56

    A. $9,441
    B. None

57

    (Air,)   (water,)   and   (food)

58

    rent   salary   interest   notes

59

60

    spring,   fall,

61

    prudently,   privilege,

Punctuate the numbers in Frames 55 and 56 wherever appropriate:

A. *The total deposits in an individual's bank account are insured up to $40000.*

B. *However, a family of three could have as much as $400000 in deposits insured by having three individual accounts, three joint accounts, and four trust accounts for a total of ten accounts.*

55

A. *The total mortgage interest for Loan #967621, which expired in 1981, amounted to $9441.*

B. *We sent the letter to 4868 Gent Street, but the post office indicated that you had moved to 96738.5 Malsbury Drive.*

56

Use commas to separate elements in a series. A series is three or more elements (words, phrases, or clauses) that are given equal weight.

The sentence below contains a series. Circle each element:

Air, water, and food are the basic needs of life.

57

Supply the words that make up the following series:

Series of words: A bank will credit your account with such incomes as rent, salary, interest, and notes.

58

_____   _____   _____   _____

No response is required for this frame. You will notice that this program prefers to put a comma before the conjunction which connects all the items in a series. If you learned that the comma before the *and* (conjunction) can be omitted, you may omit it. Both are considered correct by professional writers. However, the answers in this program will include the comma before the conjunction.

59

Punctuate the sentence below at the points indicated if it contains a series.

Series of phrases: Your dividends will be received in the spring_ in the fall_ and in the winter.

60

Punctuate the series in the sentence below.

Series of clauses: We have concluded [that credit must be used prudently] [that it is a privilege] and [that it is an important asset.]

61

62

and

63

or
and

64

The example does not contain at least three elements.

65

(A) (Sentence B has two binaries: *United States and Russian* & *more and more*.)

66

Wrong (No comma after the connective in a series)
Wrong (No comma after the last element in a series)
Right

Words that connect the elements of a series are called conjunctions or connectives.

> Ex.: 1. Pennies and nickels and dimes and quarters and half dollars
> 2. Pennies, nickels, dimes, quarters, and half dollars

In the foregoing examples, the comma replaces the _____ as the connective.

62

Each of the elements in the two sets of series below has been underlined.

> Credit is an agreement whereby a <u>government</u>, <u>an industry</u>, <u>a business</u>, or <u>an individual</u> may obtain the immediate use of <u>goods</u>, <u>services</u>, and <u>money</u> and may pay for them at some future date.

The connector in the first series is _____.
The connector in the second series is _____.

63

It takes at least three elements to make a series. Only two elements are a binary rather than a series. A binary (two parts) is also connected by a conjunction.

> Binary: The aunts and uncles
> Series: The aunts, uncles, and cousins

Why is the first example not a series? _____

64

Which one of these sentences contains a series? (Circle the letter of the correct answer.)

> A. *Buying, selling, <u>and</u> exchanging of goods as well as services between nations takes place every day through international trade.*
> B. *The United States <u>and</u> Russian economies are becoming more <u>and</u> more alike.*

65

No comma is used after the connective in a series nor after the very last element in a series.

Mark these sentences RIGHT or WRONG:

> _____ 1. *An entrepreneur is always involved in the relationship between land, labor, and, capital.*
> _____ 2. *Character, capacity, and capital, are the "3 C's" of credit.*
> _____ 3. *Housing, food, transportation, and clothing are the four biggest items in the family budget.*

66

67

Neither (In Sentence A no comma should follow the conjunction in a series.)
(In Sentence B no comma should follow the last element in a series.)

68

two (*bi* means two)
series

69

A. should be tailor-made to each family's particular needs and should be carried out in a systematic manner

(Binary)

B. can raise large amounts of capital, has unlimited life, and is able to specialize more

(Series)

70

A. Series (five elements)
B. Binary (Only two elements—*of course* is a parenthetical expression. *Parentheticals* interrupt a main thought but are not essential to the meaning of that thought.)

71

A. None (The conjunction connects the binary *unlimited wants* and *limited resources*.)
B. produced,   each,   produced,

72

A. None (The conjunction connects the binary *that earnings would be* . . . and *that the next stock dividend* . . .)
B. raised,   shorter,
NOTE: Three consecutive periods, as used in this answer frame, form an ellipsis. An *ellipsis* is used to show that one or more words in a sentence have been omitted.

Which sentence below is correct? _____
(A/B/Both/Neither)

67

A. *Command, tradition, and, market are the three basic types of economies.*
B. *Buying a home, buying a car, and buying life insurance, are probably the three largest investments a person makes.*

A binary contains _____ elements.
A _____ contains three or more elements.

68

Underline the elements connected by the *and*; then circle whether each sentence contains a binary or a series:

69

A. *A savings program should be tailor-made to each family's particular needs and should be carried out in a systematic manner. (Binary/Series)*
B. *The corporation can raise large amounts of capital, has unlimited life, and is able to specialize more. (Binary/Series)*

State whether each sentence contains a binary or a series:

70

A. *The major phases of the business cycle are commonly called prosperity, crisis, recession, depression, and revival.* _____
B. *Each person's income depends on the quantity of resources which he or she contributes to production and, of course, on the price which these resources command on the market.* _____

Remember, a series is punctuated with commas, but a binary (two elements) is not.

Punctuate the sentences in Frames 71 and 72:

71

A. *Every society faces the conflict between unlimited wants and limited resources.*
B. *Every society has to develop an economic system to determine <u>what</u> type of goods should be produced <u>how much</u> of each <u>how</u> these goods should be produced and <u>for whom</u>.*

A. *The board of directors decided that earnings would be used for further capital expansion and that the next stock dividend would be double.*
B. *Our union argued that wages should be raised that the work week should be shorter and that more fringe benefits should be included in the pay package.*

72

73

before and after

74

Ⓑ (Sentence A should have a comma after the word *etc.*)

75 Yes. A comma always precedes the word *etc.*; no comma can follow a period at the end of a sentence.

76

Ⓐ and Ⓑ

77 Neither (A and B are both incorrect. In Sentence A no comma should follow the last item in a series. In Sentence B either the *ands* or the commas should be omitted—one connective is sufficient.)

78 In the metric system/the kilogram measures weight, the meter measures distance, ~~and~~ the liter measures volume, and/degrees Celsius measures temperature.

If a series contains the word *etc.*, commas are placed around (before and after) this abbreviation to show that the series continues in thought. An *etc.* that ends a sentence can have a comma only before it, of course.

> Ex.: 1. In a technological society special training, knowledge, skills, <u>etc.</u>, are usually rewarded by increased income.
> 2. Although tariffs affect prices, labor, agriculture, <u>etc.</u>, a reduction in them would adversely affect certain industries.

> *In the first example, the etc. indicates that there are several more elements in the series; therefore, a comma is placed both _____ and _____ the word* etc.

73

Etc. stands for "and so forth."

Which phrase is correct? (Circle the letter of the correct answer.)

> A. *Under the no-fault auto insurance plan, people can collect for their medical bills, loss of wages, property damage, etc. from their own insurance company.*
> B. *We bought a refrigerator, stove, couch, chair, etc., when we first moved in.*

74

Is the sentence below correct? _____ Why? _____

> *The equipment included radio, tires, heater, etc.*

75

When the connectives are left in the sentence, no commas are necessary since the commas take the place of connectives. (See Frame 62.)

Which of the sentences in Frames 76 and 77 are punctuated correctly? (Circle the letter of the correct answer.)

> A. *The United States and Russia and Japan and West Germany are the four leading industrial nations of the world.*
> B. *The president opened the letter, read the contents, consulted the vice-president, and called an emergency meeting.*

76

> A. *Savings of individuals as well as families, savings of business firms, and extensions of bank credit, are a few general sources of loanable funds.*
> B. *In underdeveloped nations such as China, and India, and Indonesia, etc., almost all of the personal income goes for food.*

77

Cross out unnecessary connectives and/or commas in the following sentence:

> *In the metric system, the kilogram measures weight, the meter measures distance, and the liter measures volume, and, degrees Celsius measures temperature.*

78

79

No.

80

and   to provide for the family . . . to build a reserve of funds . . .
_or_   needs . . . old age

81

Yes. (Either a comma or no comma is acceptable before the conjunction in a series.)

82

B

83

Ⓑ

Does the following sentence contain a series? _____
(Yes/No)

79

The principal goals of insurance are these: to provide for the family and, at the same time, to build a reserve of funds for immediate needs or old age.

Underline the two connectives in the sentence in the preceding frame and write what they connect. _____

80

In punctuating a series, you may choose either to use or not to use a comma before the connective which introduces the last item. Both ways are considered correct. (See Frame 59.)

Right: Peter, Paul, and Mary
Right: Jennifer Coleman, Mike Douglas, Cynthia Goodman and Reverend Clarence Wallace

81

Is the following sentence acceptable? _____

The director realized that sales were down, that people were leaving to take jobs elsewhere, and that the company was in trouble.

Although the comma before the conjunction in a series is usually optional, most publishers, reporters, and businesspeople prefer it for the simple reason that the omission of the comma is often confusing. Compare the following:

A. The following people ate at the Grand Hotel: Henry Kissinger, Douglas Fairbanks, Jr., Diana Ross and Queen Elizabeth.
B. The following people ate at the Grand Hotel: Henry Kissinger, Douglas Fairbanks, Jr., Diana Ross, and Queen Elizabeth.

82

In the above examples the intended meaning was that Diana Ross and Queen Elizabeth did not eat at the Grand Hotel together. Which example conveys this meaning more clearly? _____
(A/B)

Sometimes the comma before the conjunction is <u>not</u> optional, depending on the meaning. Observe this sentence:

The carpeting was available in the following colors: gold, red, tan, aqua, dark brown, orange and black, blue, and green.

How many different rugs are there in the sentence above? (Circle the letter of the correct answer.)

83

A. 7
B. 8
C. 9

84 The carpeting was available in the following colors: gold, red, tan, aqua, dark brown, orange and black, blue and green. (Now there are only seven different rugs. Do you see how the use of one comma can change the meaning of a sentence?)

85

A. and/
B. Fire, lightning, theft, window breakage, upset, etc.,

86 $15,000 by Alberto Gomez, $10,000 by Bella Stein, $1,000 by Juan Casals, and $7,000 by John Ellis . . .

87

Ⓑ and Ⓒ

88

A. money, product, pay, increase.
B. individual, a group, or an institution . . . common stocks, preferred stocks, government bonds, municipal bonds, etc.,

89

A. The sentence is correct.
B. The sentence is correct. (This sentence contains a binary rather than a series.)

Punctuate the following sentence so that blue and green are the same rug:

The carpeting was available in the following colors: gold red tan aqua dark brown orange and black blue and green.

84

Cross out or insert commas as needed to correct the punctuation in the sentences in Frames 85 and 86:

A. *The four main types of life insurance policies are these: straight life, limited payment, endowment, and, term.*

B. *Fire lightning theft window breakage upset etc. will be covered under "comprehensive" insurance.*

85

Investments of $15000 (fifteen thousand dollars) by Alberto Gomez, $10,000 (ten thousand dollars) by Bella Stein $1000 (one thousand dollars) by Juan Casals, and $7000 (seven thousand dollars) by John Ellis were made when forming the corporation.

86

Which sentences are correct? (Circle the letter of the correct sentences.)

A. *Most insurance policies are paid in one lump sum at death, or at maturity of an endowment, or at surrender for cash value.*

B. *Most insurance policies are paid in one lump sum at death, at maturity of an endowment, or at surrender for cash value.*

C. *Most insurance policies are paid in one lump sum at death or at maturity of an endowment or at surrender for cash value.*

87

Punctuate the sentences in Frames 88 and 89:

A. *When consumers have the money want more of a product have the means to pay and are in the mood to buy, production of the product will increase*

B. *An individual a group or an institution which owns common stocks preferred stocks government bonds municipal bonds etc. will tend to be affected by events happening in the world.*

If you completed both sentences correctly, you may skip the next frame.

88

A. *The use of programmed texts, television, and computers in teaching students to think will increase in the next decade.*

B. *The study of economics helps make the individual aware that a cost is involved in every action and that this cost must be borne by someone.*

89

90

commas
before and after

91

two (month and day)
one (year)
two (month and year)

92

Yes. (Either June 1982 or June, 1982, is correct.)

93   Ⓑ   (In Sentence A the two parts do not have the year <u>preceded</u> by the name of the month; it has the date <u>following</u> the month, so there is no option.)

94

March 29, 1937, (Do you see that this is a three-part date and requires commas regardless of the short prepositional phrase?)

Use commas to set off a year when it explains the preceding date of the month.

    Ex.: 1. On April 1, 1981, the company was started.
          2. Call me before November 7, 1983.

As shown in the above examples, when the date comes in the middle of the sentence,
_____ *are placed both* _____ *and* _____ *the year.*

90

A specific date usually consists of three parts—the month, the day, and the year (December 14, 1982). If the date is stated in only one or two parts, no commas are required.

    Ex.: 1. In February the organization decided . . .
          2. The last bond issue on July 12 was the . . .

How many parts do these dates contain?

    On January 23   _____
    During 1981   _____
    May 1982 is   _____

91

Although a date consisting of two units does not require a comma, many writers prefer commas around the year when it is preceded by the name of the month.

    Right: She ran for governor in April 1982 and lost.
    Right: She ran for governor in April, 1982, and lost.

Is the following sentence correct? _____
                               (Yes/No)

In June, 1982, interest rates increased again.

92

Which of these phrases is correct? (Circle the letter of the correct answer.)

    A. *The deadline of April 15, is only . . .*
    B. *July 4, 1776, is a familiar . . .*

93

Frequently a date will occur with a preposition at the beginning of a sentence. If the phrase is short and the date consists of only one or two parts, no comma is required.

    Ex.: 1. In July we took a complete inventory.
          2. On October 23 the company plans to replace its current records retention and retrieval filing system with a computerized system.

Where must you place commas in this prepositional phrase?

Before March 29 1937 the automobile had become a household word in the U.S.

94

95

Ⓑ   (In Sentence A <u>if</u> you choose to use commas, one will also go after the year.)

96

The sentence is correct as it is. (The prepositional phrase at the beginning is short, so no comma is required after 1985. September, 1985, is also correct since many writers prefer to put commas around the year preceded by the name of the month.)

97

May 17, 1776<u>,</u>

98

Ⓐ   and   Ⓒ   (A—Some writers choose to place commas around the year preceded by the month. B—If no comma is used after July, no comma is necessary after 1867 because the prepositional phrase is short. D—If a comma is used after July, a comma is necessary after 1867.)

99

A. for/
B. by/
C. January/ 10, 1883/

100

No! (This is only a two-part date. Only the year preceded by the month—August, 1973—has the optional commas.)

101

three

Circle the letter of the correctly punctuated phrase below:

95

A. *During August, 1958 the United Nations . . .*
B. *This merger, which is planned for Tuesday, March 23, at 3 p.m., will . . .*

Punctuate if necessary:

96

By September 1985 we plan to have replaced most of our depreciated equipment.

If a date has three parts or more, commas are required between the parts and to set off the year.

Ex.: On Saturday, May 20, 1979, General Assembly won the Triple Crown.

97

Punctuate this sentence:

Adam Smith's Wealth of Nations *was published on May 17, 1776 the year of the Declaration of Independence.*

Which sentences could be considered correct? (Circle the letter of the correct sentences.)

98

A. *In July, 1867, the government purchased Alaska.*
B. *In July 1867, the government purchased Alaska.*
C. *In July 1867 the government purchased Alaska.*
D. *In July, 1867 the government purchased Alaska.*

Cross out any unnecessary commas:

99

A. *The meeting is scheduled for, January 17.*
B. *She should finish by, June 7, 1984, if possible.*
C. *We have been in business since January, 10, 1883,.*

Would the following sentence be considered correct? _____

100

(Yes/No)

December, 28, is my birthday.

When you write the date at the top of a letter, place a comma between the day and the year.

Ex.: November 22, 1985

101

The date at the beginning of a letter consists of _____ parts, but no comma follows the year in this case.

102

A. No punctuation is required. (Commas around ,1818, and ,1867, are optional.)
B. Thursday, July 9, 1981, (This date consists of four parts.)
C. June 25, 1983, (This is a three-part date.)

103

commas
state or country

104

(B)   (Sentence A should have a comma after Florida.)

105

There should be a comma after North Carolina. (A comma is placed after the state as well as between the city and state.)

106

Las Vegas, Nevada, and Los Angeles, California, (Did you remember to put commas both before and after the state?)

107

two

108

(C)   (In Sentence A there should be a comma after Chattanooga, but no comma should separate the two-letter state abbreviation and the ZIP Code. In Sentence B the two-letter state abbreviation and the ZIP Code should be one unit.)

Punctuate the following sentences:

    A. *In March 1818 Karl Marx was born; he published* Das Kapital *in September 1867 and* The Communist Manifesto *in 1848.*
    B. *The plane arrived on Thursday July 9 1981 at 8:30 a.m.*
    C. *Be sure to put June 25 1983 on your calendar.*

If you missed A, B, or C, go back and carefully reread Frames 91, 92, and 97.

102

Use commas to set off the name of the state or country when the name of the city precedes it.

    Ex.: 1. Atlanta, Georgia, is the home of the Braves.
          2. This summer I shall visit Osaka, Japan, showcase of the East.

As shown in the above examples, _____ are placed around the name of the _____ or _____ when the name of the city precedes it.

103

Which sentence is correct? (Circle the letter of the correct answer.)

    A. *St. Augustine, Florida is the oldest city in North America.*
    B. *Muncie, Indiana, is the home of Ball State University.*

104

Students usually remember the comma between the city and state, but they tend to forget the comma after the state.

What is wrong with this sentence?

    Orville and Wilbur Wright built their first airplane at Kitty Hawk, North Carolina in 1903. _____

105

Punctuate this sentence:

    Las Vegas Nevada and Los Angeles California are two very interesting cities to visit.

106

The ZIP Code is considered the same unit as the name of the state; thus no comma should separate the state and ZIP Code.

        2412 State Street
        Fargo, ND   58101-2310

How many units make up the last line in the above address? _____

107

Each of these is the last line of a letter address. Which is correct? (Circle the letter of the correct answer.)

    A. *Chattanooga TN,   37401-5555*
    B. *Cheyenne, WY,   82001-2341*
    C. *Sioux Falls, SD   57101-1133*

108

109

No.
No. (A ZIP Code is considered a number of a serial nature.)

110

Ⓑ   (In Example A too much space separates the state abbreviation and the ZIP Code. In Example C a comma should separate the city and state, and the two-letter state abbreviation should contain no periods.)

111

A. This sentence is correct. (The commas around June, 1982, are optional. June 1982 is also considered correct.)
B. Aspen, Colorado. (No comma at the end of a sentence, of course.)

112

A. This sentence is correct.
B. This sentence is correct. (Commas are placed around the name of the state or country when it is preceded by the name of the city.)

113

A. Seattle, Washington, $102,385.00   December 1980. (or December, 1980.)
B. June 13, 1980,   2,000   Miami, Florida.
(Very good if you remembered the comma in a four-digit number, but shame on you if you forgot so soon that even amounts of money are written with no decimal or zeroes.)

114

A. December 15, 1980,   Jr.   Chicago, Illinois, $1,178
B. Inola, Oklahoma,   Platteville, Colorado.

Preferably the ZIP Code should be typed on the same line as the name of the state with two spaces between the state and ZIP Code. Observe these addresses:

1. 1262 Tulip Lane   2. Pleasant Ridge, MI   48069-6516
    Holland, MI   49423-3729

Should a comma be placed after MI in the above examples? _____
                                                           (Yes/No)

Should a comma be placed in the ZIP Code, which is a nine-digit number? _____
                                                                   (Yes/No)

109

In addressing mail in the 1980's, leave two to five spaces between the state abbreviation and the ZIP Code—preferably <u>two</u> spaces as shown throughout this text.

Which of the following examples is correct? (Circle the letter of the correct answer.)

A. *Boston, MA   02129-4763*
B. *Portsmouth, RI 02871-0051*
C. *Deville L.A.   71328-2317*

110

Delete and add commas as necessary in the sentences in Frames 111 and 112:

A. *A June, 1982, issue of* The New York Times *listed Anchorage, Alaska, as the nation's leading metropolitan area for the year 1982.*
B. *We could not help falling in love with Aspen Colorado,.*

111

A. *For our vacation we started for Montreal, Canada, on Monday, August 12.*
B. *Braniff International Airlines has nonstop service from the Dallas-Fort Worth Airport to Amsterdam, Netherlands, and Paris, France.*

112

Punctuate the sentences in Frames 113 and 114: (Watch for review.)

A. *The proposed budget for the organization based in Seattle Washington amounted to $102385.00 and was approved in December 1980*
B. *On June 13 1980 over 2000 people were enjoying the beach in Miami Florida*

113

A. *On December 15 1980 Brett Hill, Jr, whose address is 308 Oak Street, Chicago Illinois won $1178 in prizes on a talent show held at the University of Southern Illinois.*
B. *In June 1981 many anti-nuclear power protestors demonstrated at nuclear power plants near Inola Oklahoma and Platteville Colorado*

114

115

(President)

116 comma

117
Mr. Arnold S. Richilieu, Office Manager
Larsen-Forbes, Inc.
13827 Kroehler Place
Waterbury, CT 06701-2221
(Notice that the only punctuation at the end of the lines is in the abbreviation.)

118 Ⓑ

119
commas
before and after

120
A. Ms. Carolyn Gentry, department coordinator,
B. Professor Linda I. Goodlad, Dean (Of course, a title that precedes a person's name is not
    set off with commas.)

121
Yes. (Unless the title is the end of the sentence)
No. (If you said yes, reread Frames 115 and 117.)

If you are writing to a specific person at a company, you should include that person's title in the inside address.

Ex.: Mrs. Terri L. Wilding, President
Scott Paper Company, Ltd.
1464 Riverside Drive
Elmira, NY   14901-1179

Circle the title in the above address.

115

A _____ will separate the job title and the last name in an inside address.

116

Observe Frame 115 again. Notice that there is <u>no</u> punctuation after each line of the address unless it ends with an abbreviation. The archaic practice of placing a comma after each line and a period at the end of an address has long been discarded by modern business writers.

Punctuate the following address lines of a business letter:

Mr. Arnold S. Richilieu Office Manager
Larsen-Forbes Inc.
13827 Kroehler Place
Waterbury CT   06701-2221

117

Which is correct? (Circle the letter of the correct answer.)

A. *Dr. Chang Tsai Manager (address)*
B. *Ms. Ruth Blevins, Marketing Director (address)*

118

Use commas to set off titles and degrees directly following a person's name in a sentence.

Ex.: Mr. Herb Satriano, research director, founded the CDTA.

As shown above, _____ should be placed (before/after/before and after) a person's title in a sentence.

119

Punctuate these titles:

A. *Ms. Carolyn Gentry department coordinator asked me . . . (sentence)*
B. *Professor Linda I. Goodlad Dean (address)*

120

Should a comma be placed <u>after</u> the person's title in a sentence? _____
Should a comma be placed <u>after</u> the person's title in an address? _____

121

122

Ernestine Lightfoot, placement coordinator,

123

(B) (In Sentence A the title personnel manager does not directly follow the person's name; therefore, it should not be set off by commas.)

124

A. No commas (The title must directly follow a person's name. No name is given here.)
B. Clark, professor, (The title follows the name; if the sentence read Professor Dorothy Clark, no comma would be used.)

125

title
between

126

Yes.

127

A. Francis R. Kendall, M.D.,   Tulsa, Oklahoma,   O.E.O. (Did you remember the commas around the abbreviated title M.D.? Also, don't forget the comma after the state.)
B. April 15, 1979, Jimmy Carter,   U.S.,   450,000   day.

128

A. $14,326   Wm. Bradford,   Co.
B. Ms. Alana L. Gehlbach, Ph.D.
   St. Marys, PA   15857-9955

Punctuate the following sentence:

The award went to Ernestine Lightfoot placement coordinator for her outstanding service.

122

Which sentence is punctuated correctly? (Circle the letter of the correct answer.)

A. *Wendy E. Parks was named, personnel manager, for Mattel Toys, Inc.*
B. *The promotion went to Jane Starnes, production engineer, who has been with the company for 15 years.*

123

Punctuate at the points indicated if commas are needed:

A. *We need a new_ systems analyst to develop a program for the latest IBM computer.*
B. *Dr. Dorothy Clark_ professor_ is on the home economics faculty at Northeast Louisiana State University.*

124

Commas are also used around such abbreviated titles as Jr., Sr., M.D., Ph.D., etc., when they <u>follow</u> a person's name.

Address: Mr. Jerry Joseph, V.P.
Sentence: Ms. Martha Hill, Ph.D., finished her degree in English last year.

As shown above, commas are placed around an abbreviated _____ in a sentence and _____ the name and abbreviated title in an address.

125

Is this sentence correct? _____
(Yes/No)

Have you heard from Nancy Blasingame, D.D.S., since she transferred to the University of Cincinnati's medical school?

126

Punctuate the items in Frames 127 and 128: (Watch for review.)

A. *Francis R Kendall MD of Tulsa Oklahoma was named president of the O E O*
B. *On April 15 1979 Jimmy Carter president of the U S called on all citizens to drive 15 miles less per week which would result in a savings of about 450000 barrels of oil per day*

127

A. *A net loss of $14326 (fourteen thousand three hundred twenty-six dollars) was announced by Wm Bradford president of Bilko Manufacturing Co*
B. *Ms Alana L Gehlbach PhD*
   47276 Fordham Street
   St Marys PA   15857-9955

128

129

Farley and Ritter, Ltd.
Potts, Payne, and Peale, Inc. (These three names make a series.)

130

A. Skelly and Mason, Ltd., of Dublin, Ireland
B. Cornwell and Ying, Inc., founded in 1953

131

A. Grace Sheek & Sons, Ltd.
B. Hamilton Products, Inc., and Howe & Howe, Ltd.,

132

The Justine/Corporation/merged with the Uston/Company to become Just-Us, Inc., in 1982.

133

Ⓒ

134

Harry Armstrong, Jr., Paula Finch, D.D.S., Les Baxter, M.A., and Helen Dodd, Ph.D., were all released by the Haroldson and Livingston Company to do research in Bonn, West Germany.

Use commas to set off the abbreviations *Inc.* and *Ltd.* when they directly follow the company name.

Ex.: Litton Industries, Inc.
Price and Bates, Ltd., dropped 4 points to 57¼.

Punctuate the following first-line addresses:

Farley and Ritter Ltd.
Potts Payne and Peale Inc.

129

Correct these phrases:

A. *Skelly and Mason, Ltd. of Dublin Ireland*
B. *Cornwell and Ying Inc. founded in 1953*

130

Punctuate the following:

A. *Grace Sheek & Sons Ltd (address)*
B. *Hamilton Products Inc and Howe & Howe Ltd were the two companies who were bidding.*

131

Although commas are placed around *Inc.* and *Ltd.*, no commas are necessary to set off the words *Company* or *Corporation* when they follow a company name.

Ex.: 1. Deltona Corporation is listed on the American Exchange.
2. The I. C. Rhodes Company

Cross out incorrect punctuation in this sentence:

The Justine, Corporation, merged with the Uston, Company to become Just-Us, Inc., in 1982.

132

Which phrase is correctly punctuated? (Circle the letter of the correct answer.)

A. *The Helms and Corey, Company received the contract . . .*
B. *No one had heard of Amy Plastics, Ltd. until they . . .*
C. *Melpor, Inc., seems to be . . .*
D. *No profits were reported for the Benrus and Hodges, Corporation, during the . . .*

133

Punctuate the following sentence:

Harry Armstrong Jr Paula Finch D.D.S. Les Baxter M.A. and Helen Dodd Ph.D. were all released by the Haroldson and Livingston Company to do research in Bonn West Germany

134

135

The following companies hired new resource personnel for the/ 1982/ expansion program: Pierpont Industries, Inc., added Cecilia Brown, contracts administrator; the Holly/ Corporation of Birmingham, Alabama, employed Richard Wade, Jr., administrative assistant, formerly of the General Electric/ Company; and Adams/ and Adams, Ltd., hired Percey Lipton, Sr., and Ruby Meyers as/ electrical engineers.

(Whew! Did you make it?)

136

end

137

Sincerely yours,

138

Dear Mr. Moore:
Yours sincerely,

139

Both

Insert and delete <u>commas</u> as needed in this sentence:

The following companies hired new resource personnel for the, 1982, expansion program: Pierpont Industries Inc. added Cecilia Brown contracts administrator; the Holly, Corporation of Birmingham, Alabama employed Richard Wade Jr. administrative assistant formerly of the General Electric, Company; and Adams, and Adams, Ltd. hired Percey Lipton Sr. and Ruby Meyers as, electrical engineers.

135

Use a comma following the complimentary close of a letter.

Ex.: Cordially yours,

The complimentary close occurs at the (beginning/middle/end) of a letter.

136

The comma does not appear anywhere else in the complimentary close except after the last word of the phrase.

Circle the closing that is correct:

Very, cordially yours,
With best, wishes,
Sincerely yours,

137

If a <u>comma</u> is used following the complimentary close, a colon must be used after the salutation. The colon and comma used together after these letter parts is commonly called *mixed* punctuation.

Punctuate the following as <u>mixed</u> punctuation:

Dear Mr. Moore

- - - - - - - - - - - - - - - - -
- - - - - - - - - - - - - - - - -
- - - - - - - - - - - - - - - - -
- - - - - - - - - - - - - - - - -

Yours sincerely

138

Many writers prefer the *open* punctuation style, which requires <u>no</u> punctuation at all after the salutation or complimentary close. Either way is acceptable; but for this program, please use the <u>mixed</u> punctuation style.

Compare: A. Dear Mr. Dorsey: . . . Very truly yours,
            B. Dear Mrs. Clabby . . . Yours truly

Which one of the above is correct? _____

(A/B/Both)

139

140

Dear Doris, (or Dear Doris:)

141

Dear Mr. Wallace: (A colon is always proper unless *open* punctuation is asked for. A comma is not normally used in a formal business letter. A semicolon definitely is wrong.)

142

No. (A comma is appropriate only after a first name.)

143

No.

144

Yes.

145

(A)   (A semicolon is never used after a salutation.)

146

(A)   (A comma may be used only after a first name.)

147

(A) & (B)   (Both are acceptable.)

148

No punctuation (The colon after the salutation and comma after the complimentary close would be omitted.)

149

mixed   a colon   salutation
a comma   complimentary close

In a personal business letter it is frequently acceptable to use the person's first name as the salutation. In this case either a comma or a colon may be used.

Punctuate the following salutation:

Dear Doris___

140

A colon is <u>always</u> acceptable after a salutation unless *open* punctuation has been requested; a comma may be used in a personal business letter when the first name is used; a semicolon is <u>never</u> appropriate.

Punctuate this salutation:

Dear Mr. Wallace___

141

Is the comma correct after this salutation?

Ladies and Gentlemen,

142

What about this:

Dear Ms. Lopez,

143

But, is this okay?

Dear Joe,

144

Which one is correct in the pairs that follow in Frames 145, 146, and 147? (Circle the letter of the correct answer.)

A. *Dear Dr. Piper:*
B. *Dear Lucille;*

145

A. *Ladies and Gentlemen:*
B. *Dear Mr. Smart,*

146

A. *Dear Margaret:*
B. *Dear Peter,*

147

If you were directed to use *open* punctuation, how would you punctuate this salutation?

Dear Mrs. Farnsworth___

148

The style you have been asked to use in punctuating the materials in this program is called (mixed/open) punctuation and requires (a colon/no colon) after the _____ and (a comma/no comma) after the _____ .

149

This is the end of Section 2. Take the section test on the next page. Follow the same directions given at the end of Section 1. After you have inserted all marks of punctuation, turn the page and check yourself. The final page is for your review; it lists all the items in the test by number and tells you in what frame you can find the item. Be sure to go back and look up any items you missed before continuing to Section 3. The information in Section 2 serves as a foundation for the materials that are to come in the remaining sections.

April 5 19—

Dr Lou B Haversham M D
473 Tunis Blvd
Compton CA   90220-0159

Dear Dr Haversham

May I take this opportunity to answer your letter of March 29 in which you complimented Beardsley Inc for its interest in education economic progress and social change (E) Would an increase of $433039 (four thousand three hundred thirty dollars and thirty-nine cents) be adequate for the second half of 1982 (E) We realize that operating costs have risen by 34 (three decimal four) percent since September 1981 and that we have to surpass your old mark of $38293 (thirty-eight thousand two hundred ninety-three dollars), set in 1980 by Mrs Dianna Langdon of the B G S (E)

May I make a surprise announcement (E) The Thompson Ramo and Wooldridge Co in Redondo Beach California has stated that it is prepared to match our donations dollar for dollar (E) Wow (E) Isn't that something (E) Flournoy Bros The Evans Corp and Westport Ltd. are also likely to follow suit after September 7 1981 if their cost-price factor stays at 47 (four decimal seven) (E) This word came to us recently from T Scott president Chase Manhattan Bank of New York NY (E)

I cannot help asking if you will please write to the above organizations as you did to us (E) I'm sure that your concern status and persuasion will boost everyone's hopes of raising as much as $1450000 (one million four hundred fifty thousand dollars) (E) Once again, thank you for your interest and enthusiasm (E) Won't you let us hear from you again soon (E)

Sincerely yours

Esteban Sanchez

chf

April 5[1] 19—

Dr[2] Lou B[3] Haversham[4] M[5]D[6]
473 Tunis Blvd[7]
Compton[8] CA[9] 90220-0159[10]

Dear Dr[11] Haversham:[12]

May I take this opportunity to answer your letter of March 29[13] in which you complimented Beardsley,[14] Inc[15] ,[16] for its interest in education,[17] economic progress,[18]* and social change[19] Would an increase of $4,[20]330[21]39 be adequate for the second half of 1982?[22] We realize that operating costs have risen by 3[23]4 percent since September,[24]* 1981,[25]*and that we have to surpass your old mark of $38,[26]293, set in 1980 by Mrs[27] Dianna Langdon,[28] president of the B[29]G.S[30]

May I make a surprise announcement[31] The Thompson,[32] Ramo,[33] and Wooldridge Co[34] in Redondo Beach,[35] California,[36] has stated that it is prepared to match our donations dollar for dollar[37] Wow![38] Isn't that something?[39]* Flournoy Bros[40] ,[41] The Evans Corp[42] ,[43] and Westport,[44] Ltd.[45] are also likely to follow suit after September 7,[46] 1981,[47] if their cost-price factor stays at 4[48] 7[49] This word came to us recently from T[50] Scott,[51] president,[52] Chase Manhattan Bank of New York,[53] NY[54]

I cannot help asking if you will please write to the above organizations as you did to us[55] I'm sure that your concern,[56] status,[57]* and persuasion will boost everyone's hopes of raising as much as $1,[58]450,000[59] Once again, thank you for your interest[60] and enthusiasm[61] Won't you let us hear from you again soon[62]

Sincerely yours,[63]

Esteban Sanchez

chf

(An * indicates the punctuation is optional.)

59

SECTION 2
REVIEW SHEET

If you missed no.	See Frame no.	If you missed no.	See Frame no.	If you missed no.	See Frame no.
1	101	26	49 & 50	51	119
2	15	27	15	52	119 & 121
3	15	28	119	53	103
4	116 & 125	29	15 & 18	54	2
5	15	30	2 & 19	55	32 & 33
6	15	31	32 & 33	56	57 & 58
7	15	32	57 & 58	57	57 & 59
8	103	33	57 & 81	58	49 & 50
9	107	34	15	59	2 & 27
10	53	35	103	60	64 & 68
11	15	36	103 & 105	61	2 & 4
12	138 & 149	37	2 & 4	62	32 & 33
13	91 — 93	38	6 & 7	63	136 & 137
14	129	39	10 & 38		
15	15	40	15		
16	129	41	57 & 60		
17	57 & 60	42	15		
18	57 & 81	43	57 & 59		
19	32 & 33	44	129		
20	49 & 50	45	129		
21	25	46	90 & 91		
22	10 & 36	47	90 & 97		
23	25	48	25		
24	91 — 93	49	2 & 4		
25	91 — 93	50	15		

Please turn to page 209 to record Section 2 test errors and restudy any punctuation rules with which you are still having difficulty.

Learning rarely comes easily—anything worth having is worth working for.

SECTION 3

Application Summary

. . . **Comma** after an introductory dependent clause
. . . **Commas** around a light parenthetical expression
. . . **Commas** around words of direct address
. . . **Comma** after an introductory (linking) expression

150

2 (Read Clause 1. Does it express a complete thought? No. Then read Clause 2. Does it express a complete thought? Yes.)

151

Ⓑ

152

(We will go to the park with you) if you will return before 5 p.m.

153

You should always ask   if you don't understand something.

154

independent   can
complete

155

A. As West Germany has so dynamically proved,

B. if you prefer a live demonstration.

156

Ⓐ

Both dependent and independent clauses can contain a subject and a verb, but only the independent clause will express a complete thought. A dependent clause "depends" on the rest of the sentence for its meaning.

Which part of the following sentence is independent? _____

(1/2)

150

          1   2
[When a bank makes a loan],   [it creates new money].

Which clause is incomplete (dependent) in meaning? (Circle the letter of the correct answer.)

151

   A. *You are careless in your spending habits*
   B. *Because of your careless spending habits*

Underline the dependent clause and circle the independent clause in the sentence below:

152

   [*We will go to the park with you*]   [*if you will return before 5 p.m.*]

Independent clauses are also called *main* clauses. Since the dependent clause will always depend upon the independent clause for its full meaning, the independent clause is the main clause.

Underline the main clause once and the dependent clause twice:

153

   [*You should always ask*]   [*if you don't understand something*].

Main clauses and _____ clauses are the same thing—they (can/cannot) stand alone because they are (complete/incomplete) in meaning.

154

Underline the dependent clauses below:

155

   A. [*As West Germany has so dynamically proved*],   [*a developing economy must plow back its surplus into more and more production*].
   B. [*Our agent will gladly call at your home*]   [*if you prefer a live demonstration*].

As you have probably noticed, dependent clauses may come at the beginning, the middle, or the end of a sentence.

Which sentence below begins with a dependent clause? (Circle the letter of the correct answer.)

156

   A. *Although income has increased, the cost of living has risen at a faster pace.*
   B. *Corporations are not managed directly by the stockholders but are controlled by a board of directors elected by the stockholders.*

157

dependent
independent (or main)

158

Both   (They both introduce the sentence.)

159

A. When you get back from your trip,
B. Since I am the oldest in the group,

160   No.   (They introduce the sentence.)

161

(A)

162

adverbial
comma
normal

163   A. Since I was unable to attend the conference,
B. as I was not at fault.

Use a comma to separate a dependent clause which has been shifted from its normal position to introduce the sentence.

Normal position: Gold prices can fluctuate drastically and quickly if money markets are unstable.

Shifted position: If money markets are unstable, gold prices can fluctuate drastically and quickly.

In the above example, If money markets are unstable *is the* _____ *clause because it cannot stand alone.* Gold prices can fluctuate drastically and quickly *is a complete thought; thus it is called the* _____ *clause.*

157

Which dependent clause has been shifted from its normal position? _____

(A/B/Both/Neither)

A. *Although minors may void contracts to buy, they are held responsible when they contract for necessities such as clothes and food.*
B. *If you would like to have a copy, I'll gladly send you one.*

158

Underline the dependent clauses:

A. *When you get back from your trip, please call me.*
B. *Since I am the oldest in the group, I elect myself the leader.*

If you answered the last two frames correctly, advance to Frame 162.

159

Are the dependent clauses in the preceding frame in their normal position? _____

160

Which dependent clause is in its normal position? (Circle the letter of the correct answer.)

A. *The owner was sued for tort because of complete negligence.*
B. *As I was unable to get out of bed, I didn't get a chance to stop by as planned.*

161

One of the most common dependent clauses is the introductory adverbial clause. This clause will contain a subject and a verb and will begin with words such as *if, when, while, since, as, unless,* etc. This clause is dependent because it will not be a complete thought by itself.

Ex.: 1. When the amount of spending exceeds supply, inflation occurs.
     2. If the profit motive were eliminated, business would suffer.

As shown above, introductory _____ *(dependent) clauses require a* _____ *after them because they are shifted out of their* _____ *position.*

162

Underline the adverbial clause in each of the sentences below:

A. *Since I was unable to attend the conference, I sent an alternate.*
B. *I refused to pay the fine as I was not at fault.*

163

164

Ⓐ (The word *although* is the adverb.)

165

A. are,
B. None (The dependent clause does not introduce the sentence.)

166

1. dependent   are
2. independent   are not

167

If all the resources of an economy are in use, (No comma after the word *obtained* because the second *if* clause ends the sentence.)

168

A. Unless you pay your bill by June 20,
B. None (The adverbial clause ends the sentence, so no comma is needed.)

169

A. None
B. regulations,   Samsonite, Inc., (Did you remember to set off the word *Inc.* with commas?)

170

No. (The introductory dependent clause is short.)

Which sentence contains an introductory adverbial (dependent) clause? (Circle the letter of the correct answer.)

164

A. *Although credit buying was not considered respectable in the past_ recent developments have changed our attitudes.*
B. *Your client called_ and asked you out to lunch.*

When a dependent clause introduces the sentence, a comma is used to separate it from the rest of the sentence. No commas are usually required when a dependent clause falls in its normal position.

Put a comma wherever a blank is shown if one is needed:

165

A. *When investors know what their individual goals are_ they can decide which types of investments will best help them reach their goals.*
B. *We shall have to delay the production of Contract No. 62965_ because of our increased overhead costs.*

If the (dependent/independent) clause comes at the beginning of the sentence, commas (are/are not) used to set it off.

166

Punctuate at the points indicated if commas are needed:

If all resources of an economy are in use_ additional output of a certain product can be obtained_ if less of something else is produced.

167

Punctuate these sentences:

A. *Unless you pay your bill by June 20 your water will be shut off.*
B. *The jury changed its verdict after Carlos admitted that he had testified under duress.*

168

Punctuate at all points where a comma is needed:

A. *The national debt need never be paid off because the debt is internal—the people owe it to themselves.*
B. *Because of company regulations Samsonite Inc. cannot accept the responsibility for your damaged luggage.*

169

If the dependent clause at the beginning of the sentence is very short, the comma is optional although preferably omitted. If the clause is longer than three or four words, however, the comma is needed.

170

Short: <u>If</u> possible call me this afternoon.
Long: <u>Because</u> of John's diligent persistence, he received his degree in nursing with honors.

Would the sentence below need a comma? _____
(Yes/No)

Because of you the company increased its net income.

171

(A)

172

<u>when a single seller provides the entire supply of a good or service.</u>
(No punctuation is needed because the adverbial clause does not introduce the sentence.)

173

Neither (Both introductory clauses are short.)

174

[no matter how much we have]

175

The adverbial clause is in its normal position; it follows the main clause instead of introducing the sentence.

176

Which introductory clause would <u>not</u> require a comma? (Circle the letter of the correct answer.)

171

    A. *Before you leave_ would you tell my secretary to go ahead and book my reservations.*
    B. *Once the public overcame its fear of inflation_ stock prices slowly started to rise again.*

Underline the dependent clause and punctuate:

172

Monopoly exists in the market economy when a single seller provides the entire supply of a good or service.

Which sentence needs a comma? _____
                                  (A/B/Both/Neither)

173

    A. *As it is_ I am not able to sell my wheat at the current price.*
    B. *As a safeguard_ most canceled checks should be kept for a minimum of one year.*

Place brackets around the dependent clause in this sentence:

Few of us are ever completely satisfied no matter how much we have.

174

Ask yourself the following questions: What part of the sentence expresses a complete thought (is independent)? What part depends upon the main clause for its meaning (is dependent)?

Why should there <u>not</u> be a comma before the underlined adverbial clause? _____
_____

175

Experts suggested that the buyers of new homes in the 1980's should allow 36 percent of their total budget for that purpose <u>if they could afford to do so</u>.

No response is required for this frame. Read the review material that follows:

You know that:

176

    1. *an independent clause expresses a complete thought; a dependent clause does not.*
    2. *a dependent clause that introduces a sentence will usually be set off by a comma.*
    3. *a dependent clause that falls in its normal position <u>after</u> the main clause normally is not punctuated.*
    4. *introductory adverbial clauses are common dependent clauses that need to be set off by a comma (if, as, when, while, although, etc.).*
    5. *adverbial clauses that fall in their normal position do not usually require commas.*
    6. *a short introductory clause does not require a comma (optional).*

177

A. Because of what occurred yesterday,
B. None

178

A. When inflationary forces threaten,
B. None (*If possible* is short. A comma is optional, however.)

179

A. None (The if clause comes at the end.)
B. None (A comma after a short introductory is preferably omitted.)

180

Yes. (Right: Although I helped, you and everyone else . . .
Wrong: Although I helped you and everyone else . . .)

181

(A)   (If you can, eat the whole watermelon . . . <u>not</u> . . . If you can eat the whole watermelon,)

182

optional
required

183

A. As in the U.S., (Otherwise, U.S. and government would seem to go together.)
B. No comma after favor (The clause is short and no confusion exists. Did you put a <u>period</u> at the end of the polite request?)

184

If you do agree, you'd better reread Frame 180.

177

Punctuate the dependent clauses in the sentences in Frames 177, 178, and 179:

A. *Because of what occurred yesterday today is different.*
B. *Tomorrow will be different because of what we do today.*

178

A. *When inflationary forces threaten the Federal Reserve Board tightens credit.*
B. *If possible see me before you leave.*

179

A. *An investor cannot expect safety of principal if a high rate of return is desired.*
B. *As you know I have already made a commitment.*

180

Even a short introductory clause should have a comma if the sentence could cause confusion or delay in understanding without a comma.

Wrong: Unless you do the chores of the organization will not get done.
Right: Unless you do, the chores of the organization will not get done.

Would the following short introductory clause need a comma? _____
                                                                        (Yes/No)

Although I helped you and everyone else were certainly instrumental.

181

Circle the letter of the sentence with the short introductory clause that would be confusing without a comma:

A. *If you can eat the whole watermelon because I don't have room for it in the refrigerator.*
B. *After college I am planning to work as an accountant.*

182

The comma after a short introductory clause is _____.
                                                        (required/optional)

The comma after a short introductory clause that could cause confusion is _____.
                                                                        (required/optional)

183

Punctuate the following sentences:

A. *As in the U.S. government plays a very important role in the economy.*
B. *As a favor would you mind picking up my dry cleaning on your way.*

184

Do you agree with the punctuation in the sentence below? _____

If bad children in Poland are punished by their parents just like everywhere else.

185

If bad, children in Poland are punished by their parents just like everywhere else.

186

ing
to
long

187

A. Having already seen the play three times,
B. To alleviate the hazard of uncontrolled monopolies,

188

(B)   (A comma is needed after recession because the sentence has a long series of prepo-sitional phrases.)

189

(A)

190

When a baby is born, families often take out an insurance policy to provide funds for college. (Did you remember the comma after the introductory adverbial clause?)

What could you do to improve the punctuation of the sentence in the preceding frame? (Hint: One comma is all that is necessary.)

If bad children in Poland are punished by their parents just like everywhere else.

185

Other types of dependent clauses should also be set off by a comma when they <u>introduce</u> the sentence. Participial phrases, infinitive phrases, and a series of prepositional phrases are examples.

1.	Participial:	<u>Hoping</u> that it was not too late, the government took measures to curb inflation.
2.	Infinitive:	<u>To</u> assure that inflation not get out of hand, the government increased taxes.
3.	Prepositional:	<u>About</u> the middle <u>of</u> its session <u>during</u> the month <u>of</u> August, Congress passed the foreign aid bill.

Participles usually end in _____; *infinitive phrases start with the word* _____; *and a series of prepositional phrases is very* _____.

(long/short)

186

Underline the participial and infinitive phrases in these sentences and punctuate each sentence:

A. *Having already seen the play three times I gave my tickets to a friend.*

B. *To alleviate the hazard of uncontrolled monopolies the federal government passed a series of antitrust laws.*

187

Which sentence below would need a comma after the prepositional phrases? (Circle the letter of the correct answer.)

A. *In a capitalistic economy the "oil" that keeps the wheels of progress turning is profit.*

B. *In a capitalistic economy during times of severe recession unemployment may rise as high as 15-20 percent.*

188

Families often take out an insurance policy when a baby is born to provide funds for college.

The sentence above begins with one of the selections below: (Circle the letter of the correct answer.)

A. *a main clause.*

B. *an adverbial clause.*

C. *an infinitive phrase.*

D. *a dependent clause.*

189

Rewrite the sentence in Frame 189 so that the adverbial clause introduces the sentence.

_____

190

191

<u>To provide funds for college</u>, families often take out an insurance policy when a baby is born. (Of course, a comma follows an introductory infinitive phrase.)

192

A. None (The participial phrase comes after the main clause.)
B. To help the business get started, (Introductory infinitive phrase)

193

A. Wondering how he would do it,
B. Since we cannot satisfy all our wants,

194

(A) (There should be a comma after *job* in Sentence B because the long participial phrase introduces the sentence.)

195

A. None (No comma should follow a short introductory prepositional phrase.)
B. None required (The introductory adverbial clause is short. However, if you chose to use a comma after this short introductory expression, no one would argue with you.)
C. A comma after *business* is optional. (Punctuation is frequently left up to the judgment of the writer; this important concept cannot be overemphasized.)

196

No.
No.

Rewrite the sentence in Frame 189 again so that the infinitive phrase begins the sentence.

_____

_____

191

Just like other dependent clauses, if an infinitive or participial phrase falls in its normal position (does not introduce the sentence), no commas are usually required.

Punctuate the following sentences:

A. We left the park early_ realizing that the New York Mets had beaten their opponent soundly.
B. To help the business get started_ each partner contributed $8,000 in cash.

192

Punctuate these sentences:

A. Wondering how he would do it Mr. Landfair made the decision to meet the crisis.
B. Since we cannot satisfy all our wants we must make certain choices.

193

As in short dependent clauses, very short participial, infinitive, or prepositional phrases that introduce the sentence do not require commas if no confusion exists.

Which sentence would not need a comma? (Circle the letter of the correct answer.)

A. Having said it_ I started for the door.
B. Deciding that collective bargaining was necessary in her job_ Gladys joined the Local Union #487320.

194

Punctuate the following if necessary:

A. In the morning_ the birds start to sing when the sun comes up.
B. Since you are_ I will too.
C. To stay in business_ I would need to hire new office personnel next year.

195

A typical comma fault is the subject/verb split. Be careful when punctuating introductory expressions because the introductory clause may be the subject of the sentence. NOTE: An independent clause must follow the introductory expression before the expression can be set off with commas.

Ex.: 1. Giving to charity is one way of reducing income taxes.
2. To rule the entire world was the goal of Nazi Germany.

In the above examples, does a main clause follow the introductory expressions? _____
Can such introductory expressions be set off by commas when they act as the subject of the sentence? _____

196

197

No, there is no independent clause after the infinitive phrase.
No, because the infinitive phrase is the subject of the sentence.

198

1. ___✓___
4. ___✓___
5. ___✓___
7. ___✓___

199

A. 9 A. M.
B. capabilities, $17,800 a year.

200

A. Even if free, *(Free public transportation* should *not* be read together.)
B. month, (This is an introductory adverbial clause.)

201

schools, believe it or not, (*Believe it or not* is a parenthetical.)

202

Both (Spending . . . puts additional pressure on supplies and prices which adds to inflation.
Most people . . . save for their future wants and needs.)

The sentence below begins with an infinitive phrase. Does it contain an independent clause after the phrase? _____

(Yes/No)

197

To collect and disburse revenues is the function of the IRS.

Should a comma be used after the word revenues? _____

(Yes/No)

Place a check mark beside those statements that would require commas:

1. _____ *A dependent clause that introduces the sentence*
2. _____ *A short introductory adverbial clause*
3. _____ *A dependent clause that falls in its normal position*
4. _____ *A short introductory clause that would cause confusion*
5. _____ *A long introductory adverbial clause*
6. _____ *An if clause (adverbial) that ends the sentence*
7. _____ *A long series of prepositional phrases that introduces a sentence*

198

Punctuate the sentences in Frames 199 and 200: (Watch for review.)

A. *If possible I plan to leave the airport at 9 A M*
B. *Because of increased production capabilities the average family in 1978 earned approximately $17800 (seventeen thousand eight hundred dollars) a year*

199

A. *Even if free public transportation probably wouldn't rid our cities entirely of air pollution problems.*
B. *Since most credit customers don't pay their bills at the end of the month creditors often enjoy an 18 percent interest rate.*

200

Interrupters frequently occur in sentences. The natural pauses before and after such interrupters require commas. Interrupters are commonly called *parenthetical expressions* and can be taken out of the sentence without changing the meaning.

Where would you pause in this sentence?

About 63 percent of students who were part of a study conducted in 1981 agreed with the results that grading in the high schools believe it or not had become too easy.

201

In which sentence can you omit the material set off by commas and still have a sentence that is basically unchanged in meaning? _____

(A/B/Both/Neither)

202

A. *Spending, needless to say, puts additional pressure on supplies and prices which adds to inflation.*
B. *Most people, to be sure, save for their future wants and needs.*

203

Ⓑ (It is short. Long parentheticals are placed in parentheses.)

204

No. (Most Americans . . . are overweight.)

205

Ⓑ (The phrase in Sentence A is needed for the complete meaning of that sentence.)

206

For example,

207

, however,

208

A. Social Security, of course,
B. I might say, therefore,

The word *parentheses* can be seen in the word *parenthetical*. Anything that can be placed in parentheses can be taken out of a sentence without impairing the meaning. Long parentheticals are placed in parentheses. Short parenthetical expressions, however, are set off by commas.

Which parenthetical expression would be punctuated with commas? (Circle the letter of the correct answer.)

    A. *The Consumer Price Index it reflects changes in goods and services is issued monthly by the Bureau of Labor Statistics.*
    B. *Your payment to say the least has been heartily received.*

203

A parenthetical expression is not essential to the basic meaning of the sentence and is punctuated by commas.

    Is the underlined phrase below essential to the basic meaning? _____
    (Yes/No)

Most Americans so it seems are overweight.

204

Which of the following sentences has a phrase that can be omitted without altering the basic meaning? (Circle the letter of the correct answer.)

    A. *Automation_ by using the combination of known inventions_ brings about automatic control of a production process.*
    B. *Automation has_ without a doubt_ been a creator of jobs.*

205

Punctuate the parenthetical expression that introduces this sentence.

    For example in the opening paragraph try to indicate the purpose for writing.

206

The most common parenthetical expressions are words like *however, therefore, of course*, etc.

Circle the parenthetical expression in this sentence and insert commas where needed. (What word can be taken out without changing the basic meaning?)

    I do think however that one should try to avoid overpunctuated sentence structure.

207

Note where the pauses occur in these sentences and punctuate:

    A. *Social Security of course is not adequate to provide for all of one's needs in later life.*
    B. *I might say therefore that a good writer will make the reader feel important.*

208

209

No. (Even though a complete sentence or thought follows the brackets, the phrase is essential to the full meaning of the sentence.)

210

D (A parenthetical expression leaves the sentence grammatically intact.)

211

A. is oral, however. (The parenthetical ends the sentence.)
B. Of course, (The parenthetical begins the sentence.)

212

No. (In both cases you can take the phrase out and still have a complete sentence, but the basic meaning of the sentence is changed.)

213

A. problem, as a matter of fact,   wants,   needless to say,
B. By the way,   budget, without a doubt,   (Notice that no comma is placed before the word *because* since this dependent clause is in its normal position.)

214

A. worker, in case you didn't know,
B. Collateral, to be sure,
C. foolish, however. (The phrase *for the sake of change* is part of the basic meaning. The phrase *because we feel secure* does not introduce the clause.)

Are the words in brackets a parenthetical expression? _____
(Yes/No)

209

[Without free public education] we would not enjoy such a literate populace.

The test of a parenthetical expression is that if it is omitted:

A. the sentence is no longer a sentence.
B. the sentence remains a sentence, but the meaning is changed.
C. the sentence is not a sentence even though the meaning is unchanged.
D. the sentence remains a sentence, and the meaning is not changed.

210

Which of the above statements is true? _____
(A/B/C/D/None)

A parenthetical expression can be one word or several words; it can come at the beginning, the middle, or the end of a sentence.

Punctuate at the pauses (parentheticals):

A. About 70 percent of all communication between human beings is oral however.
B. Of course if you should prefer the other brand, we'd rather switch than fight.

211

Does either of these sentences contain a parenthetical expression? _____
(Yes/No)

A. The act_ passed in 1927_ has remained unchanged.
B. The lady left_ without giving a reason.

212

Each of these sentences contains <u>two</u> parentheticals. Punctuate them:

A. The basic problem as a matter of fact is the principle of scarcity—more wants need-less to say than resources can supply.
B. By the way most families give up trying to make a budget because their budget without a doubt is too complicated.

213

Punctuate these sentences:

A. Today's workers in case you didn't know can produce over five times more goods than a worker could produce at the beginning of this century.
B. Collateral to be sure will be necessary in qualifying for the loan.
C. Change for the sake of change is foolish; to remain at the status quo because we feel secure is just as foolish however.

214

215

No,

216

A. Yes,
B. Well,   , I suppose.

217

No. (Take out the word *yes* and read the sentence. It doesn't make sense, does it?)

218

Ⓐ

219

There is no parenthetical in this sentence.

220

No cigarettes are harmful to your health.
No, cigarettes are harmful to your health.

(You see, sometimes punctuation depends on the meaning you intend.)

221

know,   Marian,   (A comma should be placed before and after the name.)

Use a comma to set off such words as *yes, no, well*, etc., when they begin a sentence or clause and when they are meant to be read as parenthetical expressions.

Underline any parentheticals in the following sentence:

No, I have no desire to go to the state university.

215

Punctuate the parenthetical expressions:

A. *Yes a life insurance company owned by the people who are insured is a mutual company.*
B. *Well if you would be willing to sacrifice your study time, you may go I suppose.*

216

Does the sentence below contain a parenthetical expression? _____
(Yes/No)

The director said yes to the proposal.

217

Which sentence contains a parenthetical? (Circle the letter of the correct answer.)

A. <u>Well</u> *the president is certainly liked by everyone.*
B. *Everyone certainly thinks <u>well</u> of the president.*

218

Punctuate any parentheticals in this sentence:

No education should end with a high school diploma, but it should continue throughout life.

219

Punctuate the sentence below to show that cigarettes are okay for your health. _____

_____

No_ cigarettes are harmful to your health.

220

Now punctuate the sentence arguing that cigarettes should not be used. _____

_____

Statements of direct address are normally considered to be parentheticals. Therefore, when speaking to someone directly, use commas to set off the person's name.

Ex.: 1. Barbara, why do you insist on doing everything your own way?
2. I have to know now, Dad, if I can have the car tonight!

Circle the word below that is a direct address and insert any needed punctuation:

Did you know Marian that inflationary pressures in the economy tend to be created by both unjustified wage increases and monopolistic price increases?

221

222

Ⓑ

223

A. As you may know, (Otherwise, *As you may know money* might be mistakenly read together.)
B. A promissory note, without a doubt, would be . . .

224

pause

225

No.

226

A. ⟨Nevertheless,⟩
B. ⟨After all,⟩

227

A. However,
B. of course,

Which sentence contains a direct address? (Circle the letter of the correct answer.)

   A. *Did you know Steve, the delivery boy?*
   B. *Could you let me know as soon as possible, Janice.*

222

Punctuate these sentences:

   A. *As you may know money is anything that is generally used to pay for the purchase of goods and services and to pay debts.*
   B. *A promissory note without a doubt would be the smartest way to handle the transaction.*

223

Students often think that every time they see such words as *therefore, however, of course,* and other common parentheticals, they should insert commas. Not so! Commas are used <u>only</u> if the writer wants the reader to pause.

Consider these examples:

   1. You are no doubt eager to see your mother after eleven years.
   2. It is therefore critical that you write to us immediately.

   As shown by the above examples, commas are used at the option of the writer only when a _____ is intended.

224

Should there be a pause after the word *However* in the following sentence? _____
                                                           (Yes/No)

   However you get here, don't take a taxi.

225

Sometimes a sentence or an independent clause will begin with an expression that links it to the preceding thought. These links are conjunctions and will come at the beginning of the second clause.

   Ex.: 1. Therefore, your immediate attention to this matter . . .
          2. I doubt it; however, I will take your word for it.

Circle the linking expressions in these sentences:

   A. *Nevertheless, don't hesitate to speak out for your own rights.*
   B. *After all, I feel that war cannot be justified.*

226

Punctuate after the introductory expressions in these sentences:

   A. *However_ real wages cannot be raised without greater productivity.*
   B. *An overextension of credit by banks may lead to inflation; of course_ this leads to an increase in prices.*

227

228

However
therefore

229

No. (There should be a comma after the word *However*.)

230

Both

231

A. however,
B. Of course,

232

Ex. 2
parenthetical expression
conjunction   (It <u>connects</u> the two independent clauses.)

Use a comma after introductory expressions such as *of course, however, accordingly, after all, therefore,* or other introductory expressions, when they are used as conjunctions to connect one thought to a preceding thought.

Connecting 2 sentences: Median family incomes have increased. However, in real terms . . .

Connecting 2 clauses: Under Workmen's Compensation, injured workers are entitled to benefits for injuries resulting from accidents; therefore, states vary as to the nature of the laws governing this business practice.

In the above examples, the conjunction _____ connects the two sentences. The conjunction _____ connects the two independent clauses at the semicolon.

228

An introductory expression that links one sentence or clause to a preceding thought should be set off by a comma.

Is the sentence below correct? _____
(Yes/No)

However the bulk of local taxes is spent on education.

229

Which sentence has the introductory expression properly punctuated? _____
(A/B/Both/Neither)

A. *Therefore, most state taxes help to construct and to improve highways.*
B. *The government tries to spend its money on projects that are in the national interest; of course, it does not always succeed.*

230

Punctuate the conjunctions in each of these sentences:

A. *Public utilities are natural monopolies; however they are regulated by state and federal government.*
B. *Of course you'd better be fairly certain no one catches you.*

231

NOTE: A conjunction is used to connect two independent clauses or two sentences. A parenthetical expression does not connect anything; it is merely added information that can be taken out.

Ex.: 1. We wondered, <u>however</u>, if decisions should be made centrally or decentrally.
       2. An increase in prices hurts those whose incomes are fixed and those whose incomes do not increase as rapidly as prices rise; <u>therefore</u>, those with fixed incomes benefit by a fall in prices.

Which of the above examples has two main clauses? _____
(Ex. 1/Ex. 2)

In Example 1 the word however *is used as a* _____.

In Example 2 the word therefore *is used as a* _____.

232

233

Ⓑ

234

Ⓒ

235

Accordingly,

236

A. 40,000　　hold; however,
B. U.S.　　growth, however,

237

A. know, therefore,　　June 22, 1981,
B. Nevertheless,　　processing, so I've heard,

238

A. May 1, however.
B. Of course,　　help,

If the conjunction *therefore* connects two independent clauses, a comma will: (Circle the letter of the correct answer.)

    A. *precede the conjunction.*
    B. *follow the conjunction.*
    C. *precede and follow the conjunction.*

233

If a parenthetical expression occurs in the middle of a sentence, a comma will: (Circle the letter of the correct answer.)

    A. *precede the expression.*
    B. *follow the expression.*
    C. *precede and follow the expression.*

234

Almost any conjunction at the beginning of a sentence or main clause will be followed by a comma if the intent is to make a transition from one thought to another.

    Ex.: Our sale begins Thursday. Indeed, you will want to be one of the first to arrive at the store.

Punctuate this sentence:

Accordingly all those who have been with the company for ten years will remain at this location.

235

Punctuate the sentences in Frames 236 and 237: (Watch for review.)

    A. *There are more than 40000 (forty thousand) titles which describe jobs that people hold; however automation has eliminated many jobs of the past.*
    B. *The US rate of growth however is about 3 percent per year.*

236

    A. *We have to know therefore by June 22 1981 whether or not you will accept the offer.*
    B. *Nevertheless the skill most needed by a worker for work in data processing so I've heard is the ability to typewrite.*

237

Place a comma at the points indicated if one is required:

    A. *We cannot_ accept your order_ after May 1_ however.*
    B. *We will help you_ all we can. Of course_ if you don't need much help_ I'm sure_ that someone else could use the scholarship.*

238

239

240

Well, Nancy, Maria, and Mike, just to name a few, are examples of the high calibre student at this school.

241

Ⓑ (In Sentence A the word *however* should be followed by a comma.)

242

Both

243

No.

244

A. Your order, we can assure you, Mr. Bonn,
B. I do, of course, consequently,
C. Are you ready for college, Barbara?

In one of these sentences the writer did not intend for the reader to pause. In which one would you think commas most likely should <u>not</u> be used? (Circle the letter of the correct answer.)

    A. Therefore_ I am forced to void the contract.
    B. We_ therefore_ ask that you refrain from dumping debris into our rivers, lakes, and streams.
    C. We decided_ therefore_ that yours was the best offer.

239

Punctuate this sentence:

    Well Nancy Maria and Mike just to name a few are examples of the high calibre student at this school.

240

Which sentence is correctly punctuated? (Circle the letter of the correct answer.)

    A. Indeed, her modesty was overwhelming; however I could see that she was embarrassed.
    B. Yes, I did check with the superintendent, Bill.

241

Which of the sentences below is correct? _____
                                      (A/B/Neither/Both)

    A. Yes, two-thirds of the world's people, I'm sorry to say, live in underdeveloped countries.
    B. Fortunately, I might add, Henry, world production rose 6 percent last year.

242

Should the following sentence have a comma at the point indicated? _____
                                          (Yes/No)

    Be sure to let us know_ if you think you will be able to go.
See Frames 165 and 166 if you don't remember.

243

Punctuate the following sentences:

    A. Your order we can assure you Mr Bonn will take the top priority on our list.
    B. I do of course try to avoid starting a business letter with I; consequently a you attitude is achieved.
    C. Are you ready for college Barbara

244

This is the end of Section 3. How are you doing so far? If you find that after working on the material for a long period of time, you can't concentrate, you should stop for a while and do something else. When you return to the material, you may then find that you are ready to pursue your self-teaching with renewed vigor.

Take the section test on the next page. After you have inserted all marks of punctuation, turn the page and check yourself. The final page is for your review; it lists all the items in the test by number and tells you in what frame you can find the item. These section tests not only let you check yourself on the material in the immediate section, but they also review all the material in previous sections. Be sure to go back and look up any items that you missed before continuing to Section 4.

January 8 19—

Mr Albert M Brandon Sr
19 Park Ave
El Paso TX   79910-1079

Dear Mr Brandon

Would you like to earn up to 9400 (nine thousand four hundred dollars) a year more than you now earn (E) Of course you would (E) If you are like most people you probably and quite justifiably so have already considered taking a second job (E) May I suggest an excellent course of action (E)

Robbins and Porter Inc of Miami Florida are looking for bright sensible and ambitious individuals who enjoy meeting people to work as part-time sales representatives (E) Since you are already involved in selling you would I'm almost positive enjoy affiliating with our organization (E) The job however would require a minimum of 20 hours per week if you have hopes of achieving such a lofty goal as $9000-$10000 (nine thousand-ten thousand dollars) a year (E) Are you still interested (E)

We feel that you Mr Brandon have the necessary background skills experience and motivation to succeed (E) Because of this confidence we are taking the liberty of sending to you, with no charge of course the enclosed book titled *Moonlight Selling as an Avocation* (E) Read the book carefully decide if the ideas appeal to you and return the postcard at the back (E) Once you have finished reading this material you will I think want to know more about the Robbins and Porter Company (E) Naturally after you have returned the card as I'm sure you will we will send you the necessary information to start the ball rolling toward a brilliant hobby or perhaps even a career for you (E)

As July 22 1984 is the deadline for selecting our team of experts don't delay if you think you might be interested (E) Of course you may have further questions before committing yourself (E) If so just ask (E) We will I can assure you do everything to convince you that your future looks nothing but bright (E) Won't you send in the postcard now (E)

Cordially yours

Carrie St. James

nlf

Enclosure

January 8,[1] 19—

Mr.[2] Albert M.[3] Brandon,[4] Sr.[5]
19 Park Ave.[6]
El Paso,[7] TX   79910-1079[8]

Dear Mr.[9] Brandon:[10]

   Would you like to earn up to $9,[11]400 a year more than you now
earn?[12] Of course[13] you would!*[14] If you are like most people,[15] you probably,[16]
and quite justifiably so,[17] have already considered taking a second job.[18]
May I suggest an excellent course of action![19]

   Robbins and Porter,[20] Inc.,[21] [22] of Miami,[23] Florida,[24] are looking for
bright,[25] sensible,[26]* and ambitious individuals who enjoy meeting people to
work as part-time sales representatives.[27] Since you are already involved in selling,[28] you would,[29] I'm almost positive,[30] enjoy affiliating with our
organization.[31] The job,[32] however,[33] would require a minimum of 20 hours per
week[34] if you have hopes of achieving such a lofty goal as $9,[35]000-$10,000 a
year.[36] Are you still interested?[37]

   We feel that you,[38] Mr.[39] Brandon,[40] have the necessary background,[41]
skills,[42] experience,[43]* and motivation to succeed.[44] Because of this confidence,[45]* we are taking the liberty of sending to you, with no charge,[46] of
course,[47] the enclosed book titled *Moonlight Selling as an Avocation.*[48] Read the book carefully,[49] decide if the ideas appeal to you,[50]*
and return the postcard at the back.[51] Once you have finished reading
this material,[52] you will,[53] I think,[54] want to know more about the Robbins[55]
and Porter[56] Company.[57] Naturally,[58] after you have returned the card,[59] as
I'm sure you will,[60] we will send you the necessary information to start
the ball rolling toward a brilliant hobby,[61]* or perhaps even a career,[62]*
for you.[63]

As July 22,[69] 1984,[70] is the deadline for selecting our team of experts,[71] don't delay[72] if you think you might be interested.[73] Of course,[74] you may have further questions before committing yourself.[75] If so*[76] just ask.[77] We will,[78] I can assure you,[79] do everything to convince you that your future looks nothing but bright.[80] Won't you send in the postcard now.[81]

Cordially yours,[82]

Carrie St. James

nlf

Enclosure

(The * after the mark of punctuation indicates that the punctuation is optional.)

If you missed no.	See Frame no.	If you missed no.	See Frame no.	If you missed no.	See Frame no.
1	101	28	157 & 162	55	64 & 68
2	15	29	201 & 203	56	132
3	15	30	201 & 204	57	2 & 4
4	115 & 125	31	2 & 4	58	235
5	15	32	201 & 204	59	162 & 201
6	15	33	201 & 207	60	201 & 204
7	103	34	157 & 165	61	201 & 204
8	53	35	49 & 50	62	201 & 204
9	15	36	2 & 4	63	2 & 4
10	138 & 149	37	10	64	15
11	49 & 50	38	221	65	15
12	10	39	15	66	116 & 125
13	224	40	221	67	15
14	6	41	57 & 58	68	101
15	157 & 162	42	57 & 58	69	90 & 97
16	201 & 203	43	57 & 59	70	90 & 91
17	201 & 204	44	2 & 4	71	157 & 162
18	2 & 4	45	165 & 170	72	165 & 166
19	32 & 33	46	201 & 207	73	2 & 4
20	129	47	201 & 204	74	228 & 229
21	15	48	2 & 4	75	2 & 4
22	129	49	57 & 60	76	170
23	103	50	57 & 59	77	2 & 4
24	103 & 105	51	2 & 4	78	201 & 203
25	57 & 58	52	157 & 165	79	201 & 204
26	57 - 59	53	201 - 203	80	2 & 4
27	2 & 4	54	201 - 204	81	32 & 33
				82	136 & 149

Please turn to page 210 to record Section 3 test errors and to restudy any punctuation rules with which you are still having difficulty.

Learning comes in unexpected ways when you put forth your best effort.

SECTION 4

Application Summary

. . .   **Comma** application to restrictive and nonrestrictive appositives
. . .   **Comma** application to restrictive and nonrestrictive clauses

245

appositive
Henry Washington
I

246

(an avid baseball fan)

(a term synonymous with GNP)

247

follow

248

A. boss, Ms. Spencer,
B. Hogg, an elementary teacher from Washington,

249

Marcus Conwell, a two-year-old child, won the title of International Baby, Johnson and Johnson's annual baby contest.

250

A. principle of scarcity
B. Truth in Lending Bill

Another common interrupter besides the parenthetical expression is the *appositive*. An *appositive* which renames the noun or pronoun it modifies can be omitted from the sentence without changing the meaning. Therefore, it is set off by commas.

245

    Ex.: 1. Henry Washington, my neighbor, raises lemon trees in his garden.
         2. I, Ken Wolter, promise to serve you well as your president.

In the first example above, my neighbor *is a(n) _____ modifying the proper noun _____. In the second example, the appositive modifies the pronoun _____.*

Circle the phrase that renames the underlined nouns in both sentences below:

246

    A. *My <u>banker</u>, an avid baseball fan, is rooting for the Chicago Cubs this year.*
    B. *<u>National income</u>, a term synonymous with GNP, is all the goods and services produced in a given year.*

Because it <u>re</u>names the noun or pronoun, an appositive will always (precede/follow) the noun or pronoun it modifies.

247

An appositive can be one word or several words. If the appositive merely renames the noun or gives some added information—but is not essential to the basic meaning of the sentence—it is always set off by commas.

Punctuate the appositives in these sentences:

248

    A. *My boss Ms. Spencer always insists that I not polish my nails at my desk.*
    B. *Ima Hogg an elementary teacher from Washington is sometimes teased about her name.*

Punctuate the two nonessential appositives in the sentence below:

249

Marcus Conwell a two-year-old child won the title of International Baby Johnson and Johnson's annual baby contest.

An appositive can modify either one word (a noun or a pronoun) or a phrase.

Underline the phrases that the appositives modify in the sentences below:

250

    A. *The principle of scarcity, the beginning of economics, is a very important concept.*
    B. *The Truth in Lending Bill, passed by the legislature in 1968, requires that exact costs be spelled out to the borrower.*

251

    A. Blue Chip Stocks, particularly those like IBM and General Electric,
    B. money, especially that which goes for national defense,

252

    Ⓐ

253

    Ⓐ & Ⓑ   (Both appositives are nonessential.)

254

    Ⓒ

255

    identifies
    is not

Appositives frequently begin with words like *especially* or *particularly*. Treat these qualifiers the same way you do all nonessential appositives—put commas around them.

Punctuate these sentences:

A. Blue Chip Stocks particularly those like IBM and General Electric are genuine growth stocks.

B. Uncle Sam's money especially that which goes for national defense is allocated a year prior to actually being spent.

251

Which sentence is punctuated correctly? (Circle the letter of the correct answer.)

A. Social Security, specifically Medicare, is an attempt to provide health benefits to senior citizens.

B. In playing the stock market especially speculation it is wise to invest only that money which you can afford to lose.

252

If an appositive renames or gives added information, it is *nonessential*. A *nonessential phrase* simply means that the words are not needed for the meaning to be complete and can be set off by commas.

Circle the letter of the sentence that contains a nonessential appositive:

A. Paul Newman my wife's favorite actor is also a movie producer.

B. Data processing a term applied to the handling of information in the business office is not synonymous with automation.

253

The test for a nonessential appositive is that if it is omitted: (Circle the letter of the correct answer.)

A. The sentence is no longer a sentence.

B. The sentence remains a sentence, but the meaning is changed.

C. The sentence remains a sentence, and the meaning is unchanged.

D. The sentence is not a sentence even though the meaning is unchanged.

254

An *essential* appositive is one that is needed to identify the noun or pronoun it modifies and thus complete the full meaning of the sentence.

Ex.: Our salesperson <u>Carol Sterner</u> won the Outstanding Salesperson award in 1981.

The company probably has many salespeople; therefore, the appositive _____ rather than renames the noun and thus_____ set off by commas.

(is/is not)

255

256

no commas

257

258

which one (or which novel)
essential

259

(A) Senator Bayh, from Indiana, (In Sentence B *from Oregon* is an essential phrase requiring no commas. Both sentences are polite requests.)

260

A. Capitalism, the American system of free enterprise,
B. Optional commas around Henrietta. (If Bobby has more than one cat, no commas are used to identify which cat had the kittens. If Bobby has only one cat, commas would be used.)

261

No commas are used to identify which high school. (This appositive is essential to the complete meaning of the sentence.)

262

should not

In the sentence below, the word *Eileen* is an appositive to the word *sister*, but by not being punctuated it also identifies <u>which</u> sister.

My sister <u>Eileen</u> is a good swimmer.

When the appositive is needed to answer the question <u>which one</u>, (commas/no commas) are used.

256

Which underlined appositive answers the question <u>which one</u>? (Circle the letter of the correct answer.)

A. *The novelist <u>John Steinbeck</u> was born in Salinas, California.*
B. *Economic growth, <u>a creator of jobs</u>, requires a continuous supply of new capital.*

257

Although most appositives are set off by commas, some are <u>essential</u>; that is, they <u>identify</u> the noun and thus should not be punctuated.

Ex.: The novel *Gone With the Wind* is considered a classic.

If you removed the appositive with commas, the above example would not answer the crucial question _____. It is, therefore, a(n) _____
(essential/nonessential)

appositive requiring no commas.

258

Circle the letter of the sentence that contains the nonessential phrase and insert the necessary punctuation:

A. *Will Senator Bayh <u>from Indiana</u> please address the chair.*
B. *Will the senator <u>from Oregon</u> please be seated.*

259

Essential appositives are not set off by commas because they are needed to identify the noun or pronoun they modify. If you omitted them (commas mean you can take the material out), the meaning of the sentence would not be complete.

Punctuate the appositives in the following sentences:

A. *Capitalism the American system of free enterprise is based on the right of an individual to own property.*
B. *Bobby's cat Henrietta had kittens yesterday.*

260

If Bakersfield has several high schools, how would you punctuate this appositive? Why?

_____

The high school <u>Foothill</u> is located east of town.

261

If the appositive is needed to answer the question <u>which one</u>, commas (should/should not) be used.

262

263 , Glenn, (If there's no question about which brother, the appositive will be punctuated, i.e., taken out of the sentence without changing the meaning.)

264 more than one
which one

265 This
we have to know which tape recorder. (The appositive is essential to the complete meaning of the sentence.)

266 proper nouns
nonessential

267 A. , a negative word to most people, (Even though the noun *budget* is not specific, the appositive *a negative word to most people* does not help to identify which budget; therefore, commas are used.)
B. No commas. (If you have only one friend, you can punctuate; otherwise, the friend you are talking about must be identified.)
C. , secretary in the district attorney's office, (Proper nouns will almost always be specific unless there is a chance that there is more than one Yoko Mori of whom you may be speaking. The chances are rare, however.)

268 (A)   (*My house* is specific, and the appositive merely gives interesting or added information. Of course, if you happened to have more than one house, commas would not be used.)

If Marty has only one brother, how would you punctuate this sentence?

Marty's brother_ Glenn_ is a sophomore at Duke.

263

To determine if an appositive requires commas, ask yourself two questions:

1. Is there a possibility that there is _____ ?
2. Do I know _____ ?

264

If the noun that the appositive modifies is specific, commas will almost always be used (nonessential).

Specific: This tape recorder, the Sony 355, was made in Japan.
Nonspecific: The tape recorder the Sony 355 was made in Japan.

In the first example the word _____ *identifies which tape recorder. In the second example no commas are used around the appositive because* _____
_____.

265

A proper noun, such as a person's name, will be specific. Put commas around the appositive following a proper noun, and you will be right 99 times out of 100.

Ex.: 1. Rick Howe, a good friend of mine, is from North Carolina.
       2. American workers, the highest paid laborers in the world, are paid higher wages because of their productivity.

In the examples above, the words Rick Howe *and* American workers *are* _____.
The commas around the appositives following Howe *and* American workers *make the appositives* _____.

(essential/nonessential) ·

266

Remember, the essential appositive must <u>identify</u> the noun it modifies. If it merely gives added information but does not help to identify <u>which one</u>, the appositive will be nonessential.

Punctuate these appositives:

A. A budget a negative word to most people is really just a plan to get the most from one's income.
B. My friend Leslie Mason is on the tennis team.
C. Yoko Mori a secretary in the district attorney's office introduced me to Michael Morreti.

If you completed all three items correctly, you may skip ahead to Frame 271.

267

Which sentence contains a nonessential appositive? (Circle the letter of the correct answer.)

A. My house built in 1928 by the Smith family has 14 rooms upstairs.
B. The house located at 125 Holloway was destroyed by fire.

268

269

A. economy, a centrally planned economy,
B. inflation, a slow rise in the price level,
(Neither identifies the noun.)

270

A. Gross national product, the value of the total quantities of all the goods and services produced,
B. Greg Kaufman, a chronic asthma case, . . . Arizona, the land of sunshine,

271

judgment

272

Ⓑ

273

Line 1—credit (It renames *term*. It is essential to identify which term, so no commas are used.)
2 and 3—, a service for which a consumer pays,
4 and 5—, especially one that could cause bankruptcy,
7 and 8—"What is the real cost of this loan to me?" (This appositive identifies what question you are speaking of; therefore, it is not set off by commas.)

If you completed this frame correctly, pat yourself on the back; you really do understand appositives.

Punctuate the appositives in these sentences:

    A. *The Russian economy a centrally planned economy operates under a five-year plan.*
    B. *Creeping inflation a slow rise in the price level is not dangerous.*

Skip the next frame if you completed both A and B correctly.

269

Punctuate the appositives in the following sentences:

    A. *Gross national product the value of the total quantities of all the goods and services produced can be measured in current prices.*
    B. *Greg Kaufman a chronic asthma case has to go to Arizona the land of sunshine every year.*

270

Sometimes an essential appositive with just a slight change in wording can be made non-essential and vice versa. Only by reading the sentence carefully for its full meaning can you tell whether the appositive is needed for complete meaning. In other words, punctuation is often determined by _____.

                         (rule/judgment)

271

Which sentence has a nonessential appositive that should be set off with commas? (Circle the letter of the correct answer.)

    A. *My cousin Hazel Morrison lives in Milwaukee, Wisconsin.*
    B. *Hazel Morrison my cousin lives in Milwaukee, Wisconsin.*

272

There are <u>four</u> appositives in the following paragraph.

    1. Underline the four appositives.
    2. Insert the necessary commas.

(Be careful because some appositives may be essential.)

  1   *The term credit means the present use of future income. It allows the consumer*
  2 *to have the use of goods and services before actually paying for them. Credit a*
  3 *service for which a consumer pays can be used only in amounts that can comfortably*
  4 *be repaid out of future income. A person should never incur a debt especially one*
  5 *that could cause bankruptcy unless there is a clear way to repay the debt. Credit*
  6 *is a privilege, and the way to use it wisely is to shop around for a loan. The*
  7 *consumer gains protection by asking the question "What is the real cost of this*
  8 *loan to me?" In deciding whether to charge items, the consumer must determine if*
  9 *it is less expensive to pay cash. Yes, knowing the cost of credit contributes to*
 10 *using it wisely.*

273

274

will not
will
(Nonessential means you can take the material out by placing commas around the unneeded phrase or clause.)

275

B

276

No. 1 (Do you see that in the second example the clause is needed to identify which old car sells for $400?)

277

No.
No. (We are not saying that all students do not have to take the final exam, only those who had an A on the last test.)

278

A. whose annual per capita income is substandard.
B. , which has needed painting for years,

Another type of dependent clause is the adjective clause. Like the appositive, it can be either essential or nonessential. Although nonessential clauses are certainly not limited to adjective clauses, these are the <u>toughies</u> that generally give students so much trouble.

An essential clause _____ require commas.
(will/will not)

A nonessential clause _____ require commas.
(will/will not)

274

In punctuating essential and nonessential adjective clauses, treat them the same way you do appositives. The only difference between an appositive and an adjective clause is that the latter will have a subject and a verb and will be introduced by a relative pronoun such as *who, that, which, whose,* etc.

Which sentence below has a nonessential adjective clause? _____
(A/B/Both/Neither)

A. Maggie Hsu, our branch manager, is away for the summer.
B. Maggie Hsu, who is our branch manager, is away for the summer.

275

Compare these sentences:

1. My old car, [whose speedometer registers over 98,000 miles], sells for $400.
2. An old car [whose speedometer registers over 98,000 miles] sells for $400.

In which sentence could you take out the clause (in brackets) and still know which car?

_____
(No. 1/No. 2)

276

Adjective clauses are dependent clauses, of course, in that they cannot stand alone. Like appositives, they may be either essential (E) or nonessential (NE). Use commas to set off a <u>nonessential</u> adjective clause.

E: Students who had an A on the last test do not have to take the final exam.
NE: Mary Alice, who had an A on the last test, does not have to take the final exam.

Read the first example omitting the clause. Does it say what it means to say?

_____

Therefore, would you put commas around this clause? _____

277

Underline the adjective clauses in the following sentences:

A. *Most people live in countries whose annual per capita income is substandard.*
B. *Our house, which has needed painting for years, is for sale.*

278

279 (A) (Otherwise, the sentence would read ''All girls . . . are beautiful,'' which is not the intended meaning.)

280 B. Anchorage, Alaska, . . . $11,430, which was measured by individual income.

281
A. E
B. NE

282
A. No commas (Essential to show which students)
B. Lou, who is lazy. (The clause isn't needed to identify the noun.)

283
A. The comma is optional depending on whether or not you know which friend.
(B.) Our magazine, which is sold coast to coast, (The phrase does not help to identify the magazine.)
(C.) Insurance, which means sharing the risks, (The clause merely gives added information but does not identify.)
D. No commas (Since you probably have more than one insurance policy, the clause identifies the insurance.)

284
B (A should have a comma after the proper noun *Ralph Williams*.)

Which of the following sentences contains an essential (E) clause? (Circle the letter of the correct answer.)

279

  A. All girls who are over 6 ft. tall are beautiful.
  B. Inflation which hurts older people the worst "eats up" savings.

Punctuate the sentence that has a nonessential (NE) clause in it:

280

  A. Students who take business in college should have at least three courses in economics.
  B. Anchorage Alaska was considered the nation's richest metropolitan area in 1977 with a per capita income of $11430 (eleven thousand four hundred thirty dollars) which was measured by individual income.
  C. Automation can best handle those tasks which are repetitive in nature.

State whether the clauses below are essential (E) or nonessential (NE):

281

  A. The stock exchange_ that is located in Chicago_ is the Midwest Stock Exchange.
_____

  B. Dun and Bradstreet, Incorporated_ which is a private commercial credit concern_ is a well-known credit agency. _____

Punctuate the following sentences:

282

  A. The teacher gets impatient with students who are lazy.
  B. The teacher gets impatient with Lou who is lazy.

A NE clause isn't needed to identify the noun it modifies. To test a phrase, omit it and see whether the meaning of the sentence is affected. If the phrase or clause identifies *which one*, commas are not used.

Circle the letters of the sentences containing NE clauses below:

283

  A. The medal was awarded to my friend_ who is a captain in the Army.
  B. Our magazine_ which is sold coast to coast_ has over 1 million subscribers.
  C. Insurance_ which means sharing the risks_ is the cornerstone of one's estate.
  D. My insurance_ that I have on my 1981 car_ comes due in October.

Compare these two unpunctuated sentences:

284

  A. I bought my Maverick from Ralph Williams who is the largest Ford dealer in the West.
  B. I bought my Maverick from a dealer who is located on Encino Blvd.

Which sentence is punctuated correctly? _____
                                                                 (A/B/Neither)

285

(B) (When there might be another by the same name, the clause is not punctuated to help identify specifically the proper noun. Again, this case is rare.)

286

(B) Tracy, who is rude

287

B

288

(B)

289

A. Taxes, which are deducted from one's paycheck,

290

A. No commas (The clause tells which applications.)
B. Applications, which are time-consuming, (The clause does not identify which applications.
C. September 7, 1983, (Although the clause is essential, commas are always placed around the year in a three-part date.)

A proper noun will usually be specific; therefore, the adjective clause following a proper noun will nearly always be NE (set off by commas).

When might a clause following a proper noun be essential? (Circle the letter of the correct answer.)

285

    A. *Always*
    B. *When there is a chance that more than one person, place, or thing has the same name*
    C. *Never*
    D. *When punctuation occurs around the clause*

One sentence below needs a comma. Circle the letter of the sentence and insert the comma:

    A. *I can't stand people who are rude.*
    B. *I can't stand Tracy who is rude.*

286

Read each sentence deleting the underlined adjective clause. Which sentence is still complete in meaning without the clause? _____
                                           (A/B)

287

    A. *The representative who is a cosmetologist from this area recently moved to the East Coast.*
    B. *Max Kelly who is a cosmetologist from this area recently moved to the East Coast.*

Therefore, the sentence in the preceding frame that needs commas is: (Circle the letter of the correct answer.)

    A. *Sentence A*
    B. *Sentence B*

288

Punctuate the sentence that needs a comma:

    A. *Taxes which are deducted from one's paycheck are our way of sharing in the great achievements of society.*
    B. *Taxes which are levied by the state are regulated by the state legislature.*

289

Punctuate these sentences:

290

    A. *Applications that are received before September 7 will be processed first.*
    B. *Applications which are time-consuming are always filled out during a job interview.*
    C. *Applications that are received before September 7 1983 will be processed first.*

291
A. plan, (The clause identifies the plan.)
B. manager, who is French by birth, (The clause is merely interesting information.)
procedure, (Not any procedure, but one that would eliminate excess motion.)

292
A. The sentence is correct. (The clause is nonessential.)
B. secretary, Jennifer Parker,　　suggestion,　　(Since Ms. Parker had only one suggestion, the clause isn't needed to identify which one.)

293

294

Ⓑ　(The adverbial clause is not needed to qualify the proper noun in any way.)

295
A. No commas around beneficiary (This word is essential to identify which term.)
B. No commas (The phrase is essential to the meaning.)
C. Money management, which is synonymous with careful planning and spending, (The phrase is not essential to the meaning; therefore, commas should be placed around the clause.)

296
A. paper,　　yesterday,　　(The word *Juanita's* makes the noun specific.)
B. No commas (The clause identifies which saver.)

Cross out and insert commas as necessary in Frames 291 and 292:

291

A. *The speaker presented a plan, which could help us cut office costs by a third.*
B. *Our plant manager who is French by birth, outlined a new procedure, that would eliminate excess motion.*

292

A. *Construction workers, who don't work sometimes for several weeks at a time, have a strong union.*
B. *Our secretary Jennifer Parker offered her only suggestion which nobody heeded.*

293

No response is required for this frame. Please read the following information:

Adjective clauses obviously are not the only phrases that can be essential or nonessential. In addition to parentheticals, appositives, and adjective clauses, other essential and nonessential clauses are *verbal modifiers, adverbial clauses, contrasts,* etc.

Ex.: 1. Verbal modifier: Jesus Avilla, <u>realizing</u> his mistake, corrected the error at once.
2. Adverbial clause: Jesus Avilla, <u>when</u> he realized his mistake, corrected the error at once.
3. Contrast: Jesus Avilla, <u>not</u> Phil Samuelson, found the mistake.

294

All NE phrases are punctuated the same; commas are placed around them if they are not needed to identify the noun, i.e., the meaning is complete.

Which underlined phrase is NE? (Circle the letter of the correct answer.)

A. *All post offices <u>after 4 p.m.</u> will be closed.*
B. *We have fond memories of Lake Michigan <u>where we enjoyed many hours of leisurely sailing on the blue waters</u>.*

295

Punctuate these sentences <u>if</u> they contain a NE phrase:

A. *The term beneficiary indicates the person to whom the insurance will be paid in case of death of the insured.*
B. *Don't borrow money until you have planned how you can safely pay it back.*
C. *Money management which is synonymous with careful planning and spending is a problem for most of us.*

296

Try these. Insert all necessary commas in the following:

A. *Juanita's term paper which I finished typing yesterday was turned in today.*
B. *The saver who puts money in a savings and loan is making a secure investment.*

117

297
A. Greeley, (Modifiers of proper nouns are 99 percent of the time nonessential. NOTE: A comma always goes inside the quotation marks.)
B. premium, insurance, (Although the noun *premium* is not specific, the appositive does not identify it.)

298
will
are not
identify
judgment (or opinion)
omitted (or left out)

299
A. product, service, $2,300.
B. No commas

300
A. Carson, Inc., Chicago, Illinois,
B. Incidentally, corporation profits, which growth,
C. advertisements, misleading,

Insert commas:

A. *Horace Greeley who said, "Go West, Young Man, Go West," was a New York newspaper editor.*

B. *The premium the amount of money paid for insurance is usually determined by the insured's age.*

297

For the last time:

A nonessential phrase (will/will not) have commas around it. Nonessentials (are/are not) needed for the meaning to be complete and do not help to _____ which one. Sometimes an E or NE phrase is a matter of _____. The critical question making a phrase NE is "Can the phrase be _____ without impairing the meaning of the sentence?"

298

Punctuate the sentences in Frames 299 and 300: (Watch for review.)

A. *This product which will give many years of faithful service is yours for only $2300 (two thousand three hundred dollars.)*

B. *Consumers can be thought of as voters who <u>elect</u> the goods that are produced by the way they cast their <u>dollar votes</u>.*

299

A. *Fanning and Carson Inc., who are wholesale distributors out of Chicago Illinois will have a buyers' auction this week.*

B. *Incidentally corporation profits which create more jobs for more people by stimulating economic growth are used to expand the business.*

C. *Our advertisements which are not misleading attempt to inform the public, not brainwash them.*

300

This completes Section 4. You are about three-fourths of the way through the program at this point. The hardest part definitely is behind you. Restrictive and nonrestrictive (E and NE) clauses are always very difficult for students.

Take the section test on the next page. After you have inserted all marks of punctuation, turn the page and check yourself carefully. The final page is for your review; it lists all the items in the test by number and tells you in what frame you can find the item. Do not skip over this checking process, for it will help you clear up any difficulties before going on to Section 5.

SECTION 4 TEST

November 6 19—

Gibson and Company Inc
82 Clearwater Canyon
Pocatello ID   83201-4700

Ladies and Gentlemen

Mrs Eileen Gray a representative of March and Pembrook Ltd of Seattle Washington stopped by my office this morning (E) The purpose of the visit as you may know was to discuss Peter Sterling who was recently added to Pembrook's executive ranks (E)

This visit which was totally unnecessary really put me in a bad situation to put it mildly (E) Eileen Gray literally cut Peter an old friend of mine to pieces (E) What could I do (E) Needless to say I just sat there fidgeted nervously in my seat and even stared out the window a few times to discourage the attack (E) If I hadn't been so stunned and angry I would have interrupted Eileen who went on for the better part of an hour (E)

How could Peter Sterling who is so well liked admired and respected by all be the target of such an unjust assault (E) May I say that I immediately lost all respect for Eileen Gray to say the least (E) My assistant who rarely says anything about my business associates commented later that the episode was unbelievable (E) Yes Eileen's conduct was indeed unbelievable (E)

Because of this demonstration in poor taste I have therefore decided to give the Zimmerman Inc Account a $45500 (forty-five thousand, five hundred dollars) account to you if you still want it (E) People who are so malicious cannot be trusted with such important customers as far as I'm concerned (E)

Let me know colleagues if you have someone on your staff who would be interested in handling the Zimmerman Account (E) Of course we are looking for an individual who is a true diplomat an ambassador of goodwill (E) If you have such a person will you please contact me as soon as possible (E)

Sincerely

Lee Ferguson

agl

November 6,[1] 19—

Gibson and Company,[2] Inc[3]
82 Clearwater Canyon
Pocatello,[4] ID   83201-4700[5]

Ladies and Gentlemen:[6]

    Mrs.[7] Eileen Gray[8] a representative of March and Pembrook,[9] Ltd.[10],[11] of Seattle,[12] Washington,[13] stopped by my office this morning.[14] The purpose of the visit,[15] as you may know,[16] was to discuss Peter Sterling,[17] who was recently added to Pembrook's executive ranks.[18]

    This visit,[19] which was totally unnecessary,[20] really put me in a bad situation,[21] to put it mildly.[22] Eileen Gray literally cut Peter,[23] an old friend of mine,[24] to pieces.[25] What could I do?[26] Needless to say,[27] I just sat there,[28] fidgeted nervously in my seat,[29]* and even stared out the window a few times to discourage the attack.[30] If I hadn't been so stunned and angry,[31] I would have interrupted Eileen,[32] who went on for the better part of an hour.[33]

    How could Peter Sterling,[34] who is so well liked,[35] admired,[36]* and respected by all,[37] be the target of such an unjust assault?[38] May I say that I immediately lost all respect for Eileen Gray,[39] to say the least.[40] My assistant,[41] who rarely says anything about my business associates,[42] commented later that the episode was unbelievable.[43] Yes,[44] Eileen's conduct was indeed unbelievable![45]*

    Because of this demonstration in poor taste,[46] I have,[47]* therefore,[48]* decided to give the Zimmerman,[49] Inc[50],[51] Account,[52] a $45,[53]500 account,[54] to you[55] if you still want it[56] People[57] who are so malicious[58] cannot be trusted with such important customers,[59] as far as I'm concerned.[60]

Let me know,[64] colleagues,[65] if you have someone on your staff[66] who would be interested in handling the Zimmerman Account.[67] Of course,[68] we are looking for an individual[69] who is a true diplomat,[70] an ambassador of goodwill.[71] If you have such a person,[72] will you please contact me as soon as possible.[73]

Sincerely,[74]

Lee Ferguson

agl

(The * after the mark of punctuation indicates that the punctuation is optional.)

SECTION 4
REVIEW SHEET

If you missed no.	See Frame no.	If you missed no.	See Frame no.	If you missed no.	See Frame no.
1	101	25	2 & 4	49	129
2	129	26	10	50	15
3	15	27	226 & 229	51	129
4	103	28	57 - 60	52	245 & 266
5	53	29	57 & 59	53	49 & 50
6	138 & 149	30	2 & 4	54	245 & 248
7	15	31	157 & 162	55	165 & 166
8	245 & 248	32	277 & 283	56	2 & 4
9	129	33	2 & 4	57	275 & 283
10	15	34	283 & 285	58	275 & 283
11	129 & 245	35	57 & 58	59	201 & 211
12	103	36	57 & 59	60	2 & 4
13	103 & 105	37	283 & 285	61	129
14	2 & 4	38	10	62	15
15	201 & 203	39	201 & 203	63	101
16	201 & 204	40	32 & 33	64	221
17	275 & 285	41	275 & 283	65	221
18	2 & 4	42	277 & 283	66	275 & 277
19	277 & 283	43	2 & 4	67	2 & 4
20	277 & 283	44	215	68	228 & 229
21	201 & 204	45	6	69	275 & 283
22	2 & 4	46	157 & 158	70	245 & 248
23	245 & 266	47	207 & 224	71	2 & 4
24	245 & 248	48	207 & 224	72	157 & 162
				73	32 & 33
				74	136 & 149

Please turn to page 211 to record Section 4 test errors and restudy any punctuation rules with which you are still having difficulty.

Learning can be stimulating and fun.

SECTION 5

Application Summary

. . .   **Comma** to separate two independent clauses connected by a simple coordinating conjunction

. . .   **Semicolon** between two independent clauses connected by a simple coordinating conjunction when either of the clauses contains punctuation

. . .   **Semicolon** between two independent clauses with no conjunction

. . .   **Semicolon** between two independent clauses connected by a longer coordinating conjunction

301

2

302

Jean Jordan, [who is our top executive secretary], recently transferred to our overseas operations.

303

Social Security   gives

304

After taking consumer economics, I have a better understanding of my role as a consumer, worker, and citizen.

305

A. Dr. Frances Vasquez decided to take a vacation to Florida
B. the satisfaction yielded by the last unit of that product decreases.

306

subject
verb
thought

Up to this point the punctuation you have learned has been commas for dependent clauses. Now we will turn our attention to the *independent* or *main clause*, which is a clause that is complete in meaning and can stand alone.

301

               1   2

[If an individual wants to buy or sell stocks], [a broker must be contacted to complete the transaction].

Which part of the above sentence is the independent clause? _____

                                                       (1/2)

A *dependent clause* contains a subject and a verb but is not a complete thought in itself; an *independent clause* will always contain a subject and a verb and is a complete thought in itself.

302

Place the adjective (dependent) clause below in brackets and underline the independent clause:

    Jean Jordan, who is our top executive secretary, recently transferred to our overseas operations.

Underline the subject once and the verb twice in the independent clause below:

303

    Social Security, which is a mandatory form of insurance, gives us a way of providing for our old age during the years of greatest income.

A main clause and an independent clause are the same thing. Whereas the *dependent clause* depends on the main clause for its meaning, a *main (independent) clause* is complete in meaning.

304

Underline the independent clause twice and the dependent clause once in the following sentence.

    After taking consumer economics, I have a better understanding of my role as a consumer, worker, and citizen.

Underline the independent clauses in these sentences:
    A. *Dr. Frances Vasquez decided to take a vacation to Florida since she had never been there.*
    B. *As one consumes more of a product, the satisfaction yielded by the last unit of that product decreases.*

305

An independent clause will contain both a _____ and a _____ and will express a complete _____.

306

307

I <u>want</u>

<u>I</u> <u>must be</u>

308

Yes. (*You* is the understood subject in the first clause. Remember, this is the only subject that doesn't have to be stated.)

309

310

A. vote, but (The comma always goes <u>before</u> the simple conjunction.)
B. union, and

311

Yes. (The sentence meets the criteria.)

Quite frequently two main clauses will occur in the same sentence. The two separate thoughts will usually be very similar in meaning (related) and may be connected by the conjunctions *and*, *but*, *so*, *or*, *nor*, and *for*. When this happens, a comma is used to separate the two clauses.

307

1   2

Ex.: [I want to spend more time with you], but [I must be in Kansas City by evening].

Underline the subject once and the verb twice in both of the independent clauses above.

Does this sentence contain two independent clauses, i.e., two separate thoughts both containing a subject and a verb? _____

308

(Yes/No)

Let me know your schedule, and we will get together again when you are back in town.

The comma used with a coordinating conjunction between two independent clauses is always placed <u>before</u> the conjunction.

    Right: The business cycle consists of four phases, <u>but</u> business activity does not normally follow it exactly.

    Wrong: A study of the business cycle helps one to understand how wide fluctuations can be controlled <u>and</u>, management may be able to forecast business activity in the period ahead.

309

Given two independent clauses connected by one of the following simple conjunctions, which one would be punctuated correctly? (Circle the letter of the correct answer.)

    A. so,
    B. , and,
    C. , but

Punctuate the two independent clauses in both of these sentences:

    A. Common stock allows stockholders to vote <u>but</u> preferred stock usually has no voting privileges.
    B. Two years ago you asked me to join the credit union <u>and</u> now I am writing to see if I am still eligible.

310

Is the comma correct between these two clauses? _____

(Yes/No)

Technological change shoots along with phenomenal speed, but human attitudes change very slowly.

Analysis: 1. Are there two independent thoughts?
              2. Do these thoughts both contain a subject and a verb?
              3. Is there a simple conjunction (*and*, *but*, *for*, etc.) connecting the two clauses?

311

If you can answer "yes" to all three of these questions, a comma will be required.

312

No. (The second clause has no subject; therefore, it cannot stand alone.) NOTE: Even if you think the subject is obvious, if it is not repeated or stated, the clause will not be independent. The only subject that can be implied is *you*.

313

(D)

314

(B)

315

A. policies, but
B. No comma (The second part has no subject.)

316

(B)   (The subject is missing in the second part.)

317

A. future, and
B. stocks, and (*You* is understood in both clauses.)

Are both of these clauses independent? _____ Why? _____

(Yes/No)

_____

312

I was just sitting here thinking of you and was hoping you'd call.

If the subject does not appear in the second clause, that clause cannot stand alone; thus, no comma will be used before the conjunction if the subject is missing.

   Wrong: Wise investors diversify their holdings, and buy as many different kinds of industries as they can.

    Right: Wise investors diversify their holdings, and they buy as many different kinds of industries as they can.

In the above examples the reason the first example is wrong is that: (Circle the letter of the correct answer.)

   A. *there is no conjunction between the two clauses.*
   B. *the first clause is not independent.*
   C. *the comma should go after the conjunction rather than before.*
   D. *the part following the conjunction is not an independent clause because the subject is missing.*

313

Which of the following can be punctuated before the coordinating conjunction? (Circle the letter of the correct answer.)

   A. *I intend to save my money this summer and go to Europe next year.*
   B. *I intend to save my money this summer and by this time next year I will be in Europe.*

314

Punctuate these sentences:

   A. *Term insurance costs the least of all policies but it provides the greatest amount of pure protection.*
   B. *We checked our fuel supply and decided to drive on.*

If you completed both A and B correctly, advance to Frame 318.

315

Which sentence does not contain two independent clauses? (Circle the letter of the correct answer.)

   A. *Will your business collapse next year or will it survive this critical period?*
   B. *Your idea is good but does not take the cost of depreciation into account.*

316

Punctuate if the clauses are independent:

   A. *More people will be involved in service occupations in the future and a major problem of society will be the creative use of leisure time.*
   B. *Be careful in buying speculative stocks and don't take wild hunches from tipsters!*

317

318

No. (The two clauses are binary objects of the verb.)

319

A. None (The sentence contains a binary. If you put a comma in the year *2000*, ask yourself if the year <u>1982</u> requires a comma? See Frame 53 if you have forgotten.)
B. None (The series is punctuated correctly.)
C. None (The second part does not contain a subject.)

320

321

A. Two main clauses
B. One main clause (A long sentence does not necessarily mean it will have several independent clauses. The adverbial *when* clause happens to be extremely long in this case.)
C. One main clause (The second part does not have a subject.)

322

A. Rapid transit systems would help to cut down on air pollution/ and traffic congestion, but/ they are much less convenient than automobiles.
B. You may call me at home, or I shall be glad to stop by your office after school some evening.

323

A. I have wanted to visit Hawaii for a long time, and/ this will be my first opportunity.
B. The sentence is correct.

Does the sentence below contain two independent clauses? _____

(Yes/No)

We are asking [that you be patient with us] and [that you write us as soon as the order arrives].

318

Again, be careful not to insert a comma every time you see a conjunction. Conjunctions connect many things besides two independent clauses.

Punctuate the following sentences if necessary:

A. *It has been projected that by the year 2000 most Americans will live in a metropolitan area and that most dwellings will be apartments.*

B. *Business needs land, labor, capital, and management in order to produce goods and services.*

C. *The American laborer earns one of the highest wage rates in the world and pays one of the lowest tax rates.*

319

If you missed A, B, or C in the preceding frame, go back to Frame 313, work back up to this point, then proceed to Frame 321. If you completed them all correctly, branch ahead to Frame 323.

320

How many main clauses are there in these sentences?

A. *A good credit rating is a valuable asset, for merchants can exchange information about their credit customers through an agency called a credit bureau.* _____

B. *When a group of people with common interests agree to bring some of their savings together from which to make loans to each other at low interest rates, a credit union is formed.* _____

C. *Don Paige was the first runner in 21 years to win a double in the NCAA outdoor track and field 800- and 1,500-meter races and was compared with the great Jim Ryun.* _____

321

Cross out and insert commas as necessary in Frames 322 and 323:

A. *Rapid transit systems would help to cut down on air pollution, and traffic congestion but, they are much less convenient than automobiles.*

B. *You may call me at home or I shall be glad to stop by your office after school some evening.*

322

A. *I have wanted to visit Hawaii for a long time, and, this will be my first opportunity.*

B. *Tom's mother has not been well for years, nor has his father been able to work because of a heart condition.*

323

324

No. (A comma is not required, but it is not incorrect to insert one. Most authorities leave it out. The trend is toward as few commas as possible.)

325

(A) (The comma may be omitted because the clauses are short and closely related.)

326

scraps (At first it sounds as if Spot ate both the scraps and his master.)

327

(B) rhino, (The length of the clauses is not the important consideration. Omitting the comma after *rhino* makes one think at first that Billy was also shot, accidentally.)

328

A. The comma may be omitted between these short clauses.
B. god, (This sentence definitely is sufficiently long to require a comma between the two independent clauses.)
C. Again, the comma is optional. (The length of the clauses is a matter of judgment.)

329

comma
semicolon
has a comma
semicolon

A comma is required in most independent clauses connected by *and*, *but*, *for*, etc. However, when the clauses are very short and closely related, the comma may be omitted.

> Ex.: 1. Alicia danced <u>and</u> Jan sang.
> 2. I win <u>or</u> I don't play.

Rachael is blonde and Gladys is brunette.

Would the sentence above need a comma? _____
(Yes/No)

324

In which sentence may the comma be omitted before the conjunction? (Circle the letter of the correct answer.)

A. *Joanne is rich_ and Ramona is poor.*
B. *Experts recommend that families save 5-20 percent of their spendable income_ but most families save much less.*

325

If there is a chance two short clauses will be misread, definitely insert the comma.

> Ex.: Spot ate the scraps and his master ate steak.

Pets aren't normally that vicious, so put a comma after _____ in the above example.

326

Which sentence would need a comma? (Circle the letter of the correct answer.)

A. *Birds fly but turtles walk.*
B. *Carmen shot the rhino and her friend Billy accidentally fell.*

327

Punctuate the following:
A. *I rode but Marsha walked.*
B. *Hercules must have been a real god for no other human being has ever been so strong.*
C. *Rhoda sings beautifully and I accompany her.*

328

Another good practice in business letter writing is to put a semicolon before the simple coordinating conjunction (*and*, *but*, *so*, *for*, *or*, etc.) when either of the two independent clauses already contains a comma.

OK: If you are able, pay your account at the end of the month, and you will not be charged for the use of the credit.
BETTER: If you are in a hurry, we will try to fill your order right away; but let us know if you should change your mind.

As shown above, either a _____ or a _____ is acceptable between two independent clauses when either of the clauses already _____; however, a _____ is preferable.

329

330

No. (There should be a semicolon after the word *safe* because of the comma in the first clause.)

331

(B)   (A semicolon is needed in Sentence B because of the commas in the second clause. Sentence A contains two independent clauses connected by a simple coordinating conjunction. Thus, only a comma is required in the first sentence.)

332

(A)   (A semicolon is needed in Sentence A because of the commas in the first clause. *You* is the understood subject. The explanation in the preceding frame explains why only a comma is needed in Sentence B.)

333

Both (In Sentence A a semicolon is needed because of the comma in the first clause. In Sentence B the quotes, apostrophes, and figures are not considered to be internal punctuation; therefore, a comma is sufficient.)

334

No. (Because of the comma in the first clause, a semicolon should precede the conjunction *and*. The apostrophe has nothing to do with the semicolon.)

335

semicolon
comma

Since this program is following the best practices of good letter writing, you will want to use the <u>semicolon</u> before the conjunction between two independent clauses that are already punctuated with commas.

330

While an investment should offer a good rate of return, it should also be safe, and it should be reasonably easy to get when needed.

Is this sentence correct according to the best business punctuation standards?

_____

(Yes/No)

Which of the following examples in Frames 331 and 332 would need a semicolon at the point indicated? (Circle the letter of the correct answer.)

331

A. *Mr. Higgins will be an executive secretary_ and Mr. Lemish will become executive director.*
B. *Mr. Higgins will be an executive secretary_ and Mr. Lemish, who recently came to us from Plattner Bros., Inc., will become executive director.*

A. *Be yourself, however, at all times_ and don't worry about what someone else may be thinking.*
B. *Be yourself at all times_ and don't worry about what someone else may be thinking about you.*

332

Commas in amounts of money or apostrophes in possessive words are not considered to be internal punctuation.

Ex.: This country's number of solar-heated homes is growing rapidly.

333

A. When competition is perfect, there are many buyers and sellers; and no one in the market is able to influence the price.
B. The level of "real" wages varies with the nation's productivity, so a $1,000 increase will be worth $1,000 only if the worker's productivity increases.

Which sentence above is correct? _____

(A/B/Both/Neither)

After the stock market crash of 1929 and during the Great Depression of the early 1930's, one out of four persons was unemployed, and national income plunged to unprecedented low levels.

334

Is the sentence above punctuated correctly? _____

(Yes/No)

If one or the other of the independent clauses already has a comma, a _____ will be used before the conjunction, not a _____.

335

139

336

A. No punctuation (The sentence contains a binary.)
B. No punctuation (The conjunction connects the binary to be careful . . . and to know.)
C. rates; and (Both clauses are independent, and the first clause already contains a comma.)

337

338

A. woman; and (A semicolon is needed because of the comma in the first clause.)

339

A. means to pay; and
B. company, and

340

A. No punctuation (If the second part contained a subject, a semicolon would be used because of the parenthetical expression. Since it doesn't, no punctuation is used.)
B. March 21, 1984; and if . . . party, (A semicolon must be used before the simple conjunction because of the commas in both clauses.)

You do realize, of course, that both clauses must be independent before either a comma or a semicolon may be used.

Punctuate the following sentences:

A. A family should have adequate life insurance *and* a sizable "emergency" fund before investing in securities.

B. It is wise to be careful of all spending *and* to know what happens to the money that is spent.

C. Generally speaking, credit unions offer the lowest interest rates *and* consumer finance companies have the highest.

336

No response is required for this frame. Read the material that follows.

You know that:

1. a comma is used to connect two independent clauses at the simple conjunction (and, but, for, *etc.*)

2. no comma is used if the sentence contains a binary rather than two independent clauses.

3. a comma is optional after two very short clauses connected by one of the simple conjunctions. However, the comma must be used if confusion could exist.

4. a semicolon is used at the simple conjunction if punctuation exists in one or the other (or both) of the clauses.

337

Punctuate only the sentence that needs a semicolon:

A. As I'm sure you understand, Ms. Rance is a very busy woman_ and she doesn't have time to follow up on every customer complaint.

B. I wish that I could describe it to you_ but the simple beauty of the thing is indescribable.

338

Punctuate the sentences in Frames 339 and 340:

A. Charge accounts and credit cards should be used as a convenience, not as a means of buying before having the means to pay and people who overextend themselves financially usually pay twice.

B. Capital is the amount of wealth owned by a person or a company and it usually takes the form of savings.

339

A. A good title tells you what your writing will include but, more importantly, will omit those things which you will not include.

B. Our luncheon is scheduled for March 21 1984 and if you will kindly let us know how many will be in your party we will send you the reservations.

340

341

342

comma
semicolon

343

Ⓐ

344 A
None (The subject is missing in Sentence B in the second part.)

345 businesses; (Both clauses contain a subject and a verb and express a complete thought. Since the conjunction is missing between these two clauses, a semicolon is used.)

Read this frame rapidly. No response is required.

A comma is the weakest mark of punctuation.
A semicolon is half way between a comma and a period.
A period indicates a strong pause.
An exclamation point calls for an abrupt halt.

Punctuation marks are used to guide the reader smoothly and safely through a piece of writing. If there is a chance the reader might stumble, the writer should smooth the rough spots. Most punctuation is logical if you just stop and think about it. Much of modern day punctuation is optional and is left up to the judgment of the writer. Don't get upset when the rules aren't hard and fast. One of the beautiful features of the English language is that it is flexible.

341

A comma is placed between two independent clauses connected by the simple coordinating conjunctions *and*, *but*, *for*, *so*, etc. But what happens when the coordinating conjunction is left out? The clauses are still independent and closely enough related that a comma is insufficient; yet a period is too strong. What's left? Of course, the semicolon.

Use a semicolon between two closely related independent clauses when the conjunction has been omitted.

   Ex.: An investment that can be turned into money quickly is said to be liquid; this is
        important in case of an emergency.

A _____ is used between two independent clauses when the clauses are connected by a simple coordinating conjunction; a _____ is used when the conjunction is missing.

342

Which sentence contains two independent clauses? (Circle the letter of the correct answer.)

   A. *Business is our principal means of satisfying human wants_ it produces whatever the consumer demands.*
   B. *Business is our principal means of satisfying human wants_ and produces whatever the consumer demands.*

343

In the preceding frame would Sentence A or Sentence B require a semicolon? _____
What punctuation should be used in the other sentence? _____

344

Punctuate this sentence if it contains two independent clauses:

   Banks are operated as private businesses they are the centers of financial transactions in their communities.

345

---

346   (B)   (Both clauses contain a subject and a verb. Since there is no conjunction, a semicolon is required.)

347   <u>Automation</u> <u>frees</u> . . . and <u>moves</u>

No. (The second part has no subject.)

348   comma
conjunction

349   by the government; (Do you see that if a conjunction were used after the word *government*, a comma would be all that is necessary?)

350   Both are correct. (Sentence A contains a simple conjunction, so a comma is all that is necessary. Sentence B has no conjunction; therefore, a semicolon must be used between the two independent clauses.)

351   No. (The simple conjunction between two independent clauses requires only a comma <u>unless</u> there is punctuation in one of the clauses.)

352   (A)

353   (A)

Which sentence is correct? (Circle the letter of the correct answer.)

A. *Lou swims Loren plays golf.*
B. *Lou swims; Loren plays golf.*
C. *Lou swims, Loren plays golf.*

346

Underline the subject(s) once and the verb(s) twice in the sentence below:

Automation frees people from boring jobs_ and moves them up to more challenging work.

Should the sentence above be punctuated? _____

(Yes/No)

347

The semicolon takes the place of the _____ and the simple _____ between two independent clauses when the connective is missing.

348

Punctuate this sentence:

Investors prefer to lend to individuals or to businesses because they receive interest rates higher than those paid by the government loans to the federal government are safer than any others.

349

Which sentence is punctuated correctly? (Circle the letter of the correct answer.)

A. *Insurance attempts to spread losses among many people, and it protects the insured against extreme losses.*
B. *Insurance enables us to buy a new home or car; no one would lend money at a reasonable rate unless insurance was carried.*

350

Russia is a command economy; but the United States is a form of free market economy.

Is the sentence above punctuated correctly? _____

(Yes/No)

351

Which one of the following pairs in Frames 352 and 353 is correct? (Circle the letter of the correct answer.)

A. *Bloomington, Indiana, had the lowest per capita income in 1977; Alexandria, Louisiana, had the second lowest.*
B. *Bloomington, Indiana, had the lowest per capita income in 1977, Alexandria, Louisiana, had the second lowest.*

352

A. *The definition of insurance is to spread a loss among as many people as possible; this definition does not go far enough, however.*
B. *One does not live by bread alone one must have a spiritual life, too.*

353

354

semicolon

355

No! (If you said yes, go back to Frame 309; reread it carefully.)

356

Yes. (Since the second clause already contains commas, a semicolon is necessary before the simple conjunction. Note that the parenthetical expression directly following the conjunction is the only time a comma is placed after a simple conjunction.)

357

A. demand,
B. busy? (No comma is required between these short clauses.)

358

A. price;
B. Government exists for the people; (A semicolon is used because of the comma in the second clause.)

359

business;   government, and (This sentence actually contains three independent clauses. Because no conjunction is used, a semicolon is needed between the first two clauses. Because the second and third clauses are connected by the simple conjunction *and*, a comma is sufficient.)

360

361

connect (join, link)

Does this sentence need a comma or a semicolon at the point indicated? _____
(comma/semicolon)

It is best to pay most bills by check_ canceled checks serve as receipts.

354

Is this sentence punctuated correctly? _____
(Yes/No)

Personal checks may not be accepted for some important payments but, certified checks or cashier's checks may be used instead.

355

Is this sentence correct? _____
(Yes/No)

Money is rapidly disappearing as a medium of exchange; and, without a doubt, the day will come when no actual dollars will change hands.

356

Punctuate the sentences in Frames 357 and 358:

A. *Prices in a market economy are influenced by supply and demand but a monopoly threatens the workings of a pricing system.*
B. *Can you come or are you busy*

357

A. *Gross profit is the difference between the cost and the selling price net profit is gross profit minus operating expenses.*
B. *Government exists for the people and when a government ceases to serve the people, the people should change the government.*

358

This sentence should have both a semicolon and a comma. Insert them where they are needed:

Government is our biggest business it is a three-level form of government and sometimes there is an overlapping of services.

359

Quickly flip back and reread Frame 226. Pay particular attention to the use of the semicolon in Example 2.

360

It is not uncommon for two independent clauses to be joined by connectives other than the simple conjunction (*and, but, so, for,* etc.). Some of the more common longer connectives are words like *however, nevertheless, therefore, consequently, of course, that is,* etc.

The function of a conjunction is to _____ a thought to a preceding thought.

361

362

363

semicolon
comma

364

(A)   (Sentence B should have a comma after the conjunction *however*.)

365

contract therefore;

366

The company has lost its contract; therefore, 3,500 workers . . .

367

; moreover,

No response is required for this frame. Read the following material.

So far, you have learned that a semicolon is used between two independent clauses when:

1. either of the two clauses already contains commas.
2. the conjunction has been omitted between the clauses.

A third use of the semicolon is stated as follows:

362

Use a semicolon between two independent clauses when they are connected by such words as *however*, *therefore*, *consequently*, and *nevertheless*. When such expressions are meant to link a clause with a preceding thought, a *semicolon* is used before the conjunction and a *comma* after the conjunction.

Note the following examples of two independent clauses connected by one of the longer connectives:

Ex.: 1. Dividends by corporations are usually paid in cash; however, a stockholder may receive additional shares of stock.
2. The dividend must be declared by the board of directors; moreover, the rate of dividend is stated as a certain number of dollars or cents on each share.

363

As shown above, a _____ is used before the conjunction to separate the two independent clauses with a _____ following the conjunction.

Although no comma follows the simple conjunction (*and*, *but*, etc.), a comma <u>is</u> used after the longer coordinating conjunctions.

Which sentence is correctly punctuated? (Circle the letter of the correct answer.)

A. *The downtown stores were closed for the holiday; nevertheless, we were able to do some of our shopping at the plaza.*
B. *France, England, and W. Germany have a huge GNP; however all three combined do not equal the GNP of the United States.*

364

Circle the place where the punctuation is incorrect in the following sentence:

The company has lost its contract therefore; 3,500 workers will have to be laid off immediately.

365

Insert the punctuation mark(s) needed to make the sentence correct:

The company has lost its contract therefore 3,500 workers will have to be laid off immediately.

366

Punctuate the following sentence:

Your typewriting skill is low moreover you need a good course in business English.

367

368

wholesalers; however,

369

370

comma
semicolon
comma

371

(B)   (The first sentence contains a parenthetical expression. Remember, an independent clause must follow the conjunction.)

372

old age; (Periods between the letters *OASI* would not be considered wrong. However, since the organization chooses not to use periods between the initials, they are preferably omitted.)

373

A. rights, but   dividends;
B. No punctuation

374

A. We wondered, however,   remember; consequently,
B. mixed economy;

Correct this sentence:

Retailers buy from wholesalers, however wholesalers buy directly from the manufacturer.

368

Circle the letter of the correctly punctuated sentence:

A. *Too much spending results in inflation; however too little results in unemployment.*
B. *Too much spending results in inflation, however, too little results in unemployment.*
C. *Too much spending results in inflation, too little results in unemployment.*
D. *Too much spending results in inflation; however, too little results in unemployment.*

369

Once again, don't confuse a conjunction with a parenthetical expression. Words such as *therefore*, *however*, *of course*, and *in fact* can be used as either. The way to tell the difference is to ask yourself the question "Does the expression connect two independent clauses, or does it interrupt a single thought?"

If the word however *interrupts a thought, a _____ will be used both before and after. If the word* however *connects two independent clauses, a _____ comes before the conjunction and a _____ goes after the conjunction.*

370

Which sentence contains a conjunction? (Circle the letter of the correct answer.)

A. *A business run by one person_ however_ is called a sole proprietorship.*
B. *Almost all large firms are incorporated_ indeed_ they have to be in order to raise the vast sums of money they need.*

371

Punctuate the sentences in Frames 372, 373, and 374: (Watch for review items.)

The Social Security Act, which was passed in 1935, provides income for old age OASI also has disability benefits.

372

A. *Owners of common stock usually have voting rights but they have the lowest priority in claiming dividends bondholders and preferred stockholders come first.*
B. *The functions of money are to serve as a common medium of exchange and to act as a common measure of value.*

373

A. *We wondered however if you would remember consequently we had the Bryants check on it.*
B. *The U.S. economy is a mixed economy it does not rely altogether on the market system.*

374

You might like to know that you have just completed the most difficult portion of this program. There are a few additional marks of punctuation that you will need to put the finishing touches on your skill, but definitely the hardest part has been in the last three sections.

Take the criterion test for Section 5. Good luck. Follow the same procedures as in the past.

SECTION 5 TEST

December 8 19—

Ms Loren C Beberick Manager
Fedco Stores Inc
Springfield MO   65801-0921

Dear Ms Beberick

Last Friday I bought an album from your record department that was defective (E) When I realized that the record a Horowitz recording was badly warped I immediately sealed it in the original package I have not played it since (E) I understand that you back your merchandise 100 percent and that you will either exchange the record give me credit for $899 (eight dollars and ninety-nine cents) or refund my money (E) Is this correct (E)

Mr Horowitz who is one of my favorite concert pianists doesn't quite sound like himself especially on this record (E) Therefore I think that I shall choose a different recording label (E) I have bought dozens of records and spent hundreds of dollars at your store and this is the first time I have had to return anything (E) Obviously you carry only the best brands you should be commended (E)

Since I live so far away shall I send the record to you in the mail or would you prefer that I wait until I am able to return it myself (E) I would be happy to let a friend exchange it but no one I know is a Fedco member (E) If you have a specific exchange procedure will you please let me know by Monday December 20 (E) Otherwise I shall keep the record until January 15 which is the earliest I could visit the store (E)

I have always been satisfied with Fedco products for your quality has been outstanding (E) Fedco is always well staffed Fedco's parking facilities are more than adequate Fedco has the most wholesome pleasant and helpful clerks in town (E) I have however been in particularly on sale days when I have wished you weren't so popular (E) You without a doubt must serve 9000 (nine thousand) customers on certain days (E)

Thank you Ms Beberick for maintaining such high standards (E) You are doing a magnificent job of serving the community and even during this moment of slight inconvenience I want you to know that I shall continue shopping at Fedco Stores Inc in the future (E)

Sincerely yours

Kelly Anthony

jea

December 8,[1] 19—

Ms[2] Loren C[3] Beberick,[4] Manager[5]
Fedco Stores,[6] Inc[7]
Springfield,[8] MO 65801-0921[9]

Dear Ms[10] Beberick:[11]

Last Friday I bought an album from your record department that was defective.[12] When I realized that the record,[13] a Horowitz recording,[14] was badly warped,[15] I immediately sealed it in the original package;[16] I have not played it since.[17] I understand that you back your merchandise 100 percent[18] and that you will either exchange the record,[19] give me credit for $8[20]99[21]* or refund my money[22] Is this correct?[23]

Mr.[24] Horowitz,[25] who is one of my favorite concert pianists,[26] doesn't quite sound like himself,[27] especially on this record.[28] Therefore,[29] I think that I shall choose a different recording label.[30] I have bought dozens of records[31] and spent hundreds of dollars at your store,[32] and this is the first time I have had to return anything.[33] Obviously,[34] you carry only the best brands;[35] you should be commended.[36]

Since I live so far away,[37] shall I send the record to you in the mail;[38] or would you prefer that I wait[39] until I am able to return it myself?[40] I would be happy to let a friend exchange it,[41] but no one I know is a Fedco member.[42] If you have a specific exchange procedure,[43] will you please let me know by Monday,[44] December 20.[45] Otherwise,[46] I shall keep the record until January 15,[47] which is the earliest I could visit the store.[48]

    I have always been satisfied with Fedco products,[53] for your quality has been outstanding[54] Fedco is always well staffed;[55] Fedco's parking facilities are more than adequate;[56] Fedco has the most wholesome,[57] pleasant,[58]* and helpful clerks in town.[59] I have,[60] however,[61] been in,[62] particularly on sale days,[63] when I have wished you weren't so popular.[64] You,[65] without a doubt,[66] must serve 9,[67]000 customers on certain days![68]*

    Thank you,[69] Ms.[70] Beberick,[71] for maintaining such high standards.[72] You are doing a magnificent job of serving the community;[73] and even during this moment of slight inconvenience,[74] I want you to know that I shall continue shopping at Fedco Stores,[75] Inc.[76],[77] in the future.[78]

                    Sincerely yours,[79]

                    Kelly Anthony

jea

(The * means the punctuation is optional.)

SECTION 5
REVIEW SHEET

If you missed no.	See Frame no.	If you missed no.	See Frame no.	If you missed no.	See Frame no.
1	101	27	251	53	307
2	15	28	2 & 4	54	2 & 4
3	15	29	226 & 228	55	342 & 348
4	115 & 116	30	2 & 4	56	342 & 348
5	117	31	313 & 318	57	57 & 58
6	129	32	307	58	57 & 59
7	15	33	2 & 4	59	2 & 4
8	103	34	229 & 235	60	201 & 207
9	53	35	342 & 348	61	201 & 204
10	15	36	2 & 4	62	251
11	138 & 149	37	157 & 162	63	251
12	2 & 4	38	329 & 330	64	2 & 4
13	245 & 253	39	165	65	201 & 203
14	245 & 267	40	10	66	201 & 204
15	157 & 162	41	307 & 309	67	49 & 50
16	342 & 348	42	2 & 4	68	6
17	2 & 4	43	157 & 162	69	221
18	313 & 319	44	91 & 97	70	15
19	57 & 60	45	32 & 33	71	221
20	25	46	229 & 235	72	2 & 4
21	57 & 59	47	277 & 285	73	329 & 330
22	2 & 4	48	2 & 4	74	186
23	10	49	15	75	129
24	15	50	15	76	15
25	277 & 285	51	115 & 116	77	129
26	275 & 277	52	101	78	2 & 4
				79	136 & 149

Please turn to page 212 to record Section 5 test errors and restudy any particular punctuation rules with which you are still having difficulty.

Learning begins with the right frame of mind.

SECTION 6

Application Summary

. . . **Apostrophe** in a contraction
. . . **Apostrophe** in possessives
. . . **Apostrophe** in the contraction *it's*
. . . **Quotation marks** around emphasized words, slang, technical jargon, etc.

375

are not   do not
you are   let us
was not   they have

376

A. haven't
B. won't
C. it's
D. let's
E. Class of '85

377

A. no   (cannot)
B. wi   (we will)
C. a   (I am)
D. ha   (you have)
E. f the   (of the clock)

378

Ⓒ   (The occasional use of a contraction is accepted, but five contractions in one paragraph definitely is excessive.)

379

No. (Avoid the <u>overuse</u> of contractions in business writing.)

Use an apostrophe to indicate contractions of words. The apostrophe indicates that two words have been fused into one, and it should be placed at the point where the letter(s) have been omitted.

    Right: Does not Doesn't (The o is missing)
    Wrong: Does not Does'nt

375

On the line beside each contraction, write the words that the contraction represents:

aren't _____	*don't* _____
you're _____	*let's* _____
wasn't _____	*they've* _____

If the apostrophe goes where a letter(s) or numbers have been omitted, where would you place an apostrophe in these contractions?

    A. *havent*   *(have not)*
    B. *wont*   *(will not)*
    C. *its*   *(it is)*
    D. *lets*   *(let us)*
    E. *Class of 85* *(1985)*

376

What letters have been omitted in these contractions?

    A. *can't* _____
    B. *we'll* _____
    C. *I'm* _____
    D. *you've* _____
    E. *o'clock* _____

377

Contractions tend to be informal. Although contractions are used in business writing, their excessive use should be avoided.

    Ex.: You'll be pleased to know that I wasn't responsible for the new policy we've recently adopted. I've always been against such actions, and I'm even more opposed now than before.

For a business letter, the above paragraph probably is: (Circle the letter of the correct answer.)

    A. *very formal*
    B. *neither formal nor informal*
    C. *too informal*

378

Should you omit all contractions in business writing? _____
                                                    (Yes/No)

379

380

policy   doctor

381

A. monkey's (one monkey)
B. Jose's (one person)
C. worker's (one worker)

382

A. teachers'
B. friends'
C. birds'

383

A. author's
B. authors'
C. authors'

384

Ⓒ   (Sentence A should be drivers'; in Sentence B several dresses could not have the same zipper, so it could only be the dress's zipper.)

385

A. women's
B. children's
C. deer's

Apostrophes are also used to show the possessive form of nouns. *Possessives*, as you recall, indicate ownership.

Ex.: The doctor's policy included coverage for malpractice suits.

In the above example, the _____ belonged to the _____.

380

To form the singular possessive (SP), add the apostrophe and s ('s).

Ex.: Jack's britches were ripped in the seat.

Make these nouns singular possessive:

A. *the monkey _ _ tail*
B. *Jose _ _ glasses*
C. *a worker _ _ holiday*

381

To form the plural possessive (PP) of plural nouns already ending in s, merely add the apostrophe (').

Ex.: 1. boys suits = boys' suits
2. the cats meows = the cats' meows

Make these plural nouns plural possessive:

A. *the teachers actions (ten teachers)*
B. *several friends homes*
C. *the birds singing (dozens of birds)*

382

Insert the apostrophe in the following phrases:

A. *the authors book (one author)*
B. *the authors books (three authors)*
C. *the authors book (two authors writing the same book)*

383

Which phrases have the apostrophe correctly inserted? (Circle the letter of the correct answer.)

A. *the driver's passengers (many drivers)*
B. *the dresses' zipper*
C. *the captain's orders (one captain)*

384

When the plural noun does <u>not</u> end in s, the plural possessive (PP) is formed by adding an apostrophe and s ('s).

Ex.: 1. men = men's
2. sons-in-law = sons-in-law's

Make these plural nouns PP:

A. *women _ _ hats*
B. *children _ _ toy*
C. *deer _ _ antlers*

385

386 Plural Possessive (NOTE: The only reason we use an apostrophe after the s is to distinguish between the singular and the plural form. If the word changes form from the singular to the plural—daughter-in-law to daughters-in-law, for example—there is no need to make this distinction with the apostrophe. Therefore, an apostrophe s ('s) is all that is needed for both SP and PP.)

387 daughter-in-law's

388 SP ox's
PP oxen's
(The word changes form from singular to plural; thus, there is no need to distinguish with the 's and s'.)

389 A. calf's calves' (Although the word changes form in the plural, a real word must precede the apostrophe. There is no such word as *calve*.)
B. goose's geese's (The word changes form from the singular to the plural, and both are legitimate words.)
C. sheep's sheep's (Since one is *sheep* and four are *sheep*, you cannot write the PP sheeps'—there is no such word as *sheeps*.)
D. thief's thieves' (Again, *thieve* is not a real word.)

390 A. PP
B. SP
C. Neither! (Do you see that the part preceding the apostrophe is not the real word? The word is *news*, and the only way this word can be made possessive is by maintaining the whole word before the apostrophe: news' or news's.)

391

1. lady	ladies	lady's	ladies'
2. mouse	mice	mouse's	mice's
3. man-of-war	men-of-war	man-of-war's	men-of-war's
4. attorney	attorneys	attorney's	attorneys'

Have you noticed that when a plural is made by changing the word form rather than by adding s (the normal plural), both the singular possessive and plural possessive are often made by adding an apostrophe and an s ('s)?

Ex.: 1. man   men   man's   men's
2. child   children   child's   children's
3. alumnus   alumni   alumnus's   alumni's

Is the following underscored word SP or PP? _____

(SP/PP)

the *daughters-in-law's* beliefs

386

The belief of one daughter-in-law would be written _____.

387

What are the singular and plural possessives of the word *ox*?

SP _____
PP _____

388

One important thing to remember about possessives is that a real, legitimate word must precede the apostrophe. For example, the word *wives* would have to be *wives'* in the PP. If you wrote *wive's*, you can see that there is no such word as *wive*.

Form the SP and PP of each of these words:

		SP	PP
A. *calf*	*calves*	_____	_____
B. *goose*	*geese*	_____	_____
C. *sheep*	*sheep*	_____	_____
D. *thief*	*thieves*	_____	_____

389

Write whether the word is SP or PP in the blank provided:

A. *the senators' remarks* _____
B. *our uncle's new clothes* _____
C. *the new's best broadcaster* _____

390

Write the singular, plural, SP, and PP for the following words:

	Singular	Plural	SP	PP
Ex.:	sister	sisters	sister's	sisters'
1.	_____	*ladies*	_____	_____
2.	_____	*mice*	_____	_____
3.	*man-of-war*	_____	_____	_____
4.	_____	*attorneys*	_____	_____

391

392

A. The life insurance needs <u>of a family</u> will depend on the situation <u>of that family</u>.
B. The hiring practices <u>of the corporation</u> were highly unethical.

393

bankers' banks   (plural possessive, i.e., many bankers)

394

Ⓑ   and   Ⓓ

395

leaves'
families'

396

397

A. Girls' clothing isn't as expensive as boys' clothing.
B. Our company's policy hasn't been accepted too well by most workers in the plant. (Workers is merely plural.)

A possessive can be reversed to form an *of* phrase.

Ex.: Julia's doll   =   the doll of Julia

If you aren't sure a noun is possessive, try making the word an *of* phrase.

Substitute an *of* phrase for the following possessive nouns: (No written response is required; you may think the answer to yourself.)

A. *A* <u>family's</u> *life insurance needs will depend on that* <u>family's</u> *situation.*
B. *The* <u>corporation's</u> *hiring practices were highly unethical.*

392

Change the underlined phrase below to a possessive noun: _____

Federal Reserve banks are <u>banks of bankers</u> *and cannot be used by the public.*

393

An apostrophe plus an *of* phrase are unnecessary and, therefore, redundant.

Ex.: The doll <u>of</u> Julia's.

Which sentences are correct? (Circle the letter of the correct answer(s)).

A. *The characters of the novel's were all fictional.*
B. *The novel's characters were all fictional.*
C. *The novels character's were all fictional.*
D. *The characters of the novel were all fictional.*

394

If you have difficulty deciding whether the possessive should be s' or 's, think of the singular and plural forms of the word and then decide. You know that:

1. a SP will be 's.
2. a PP will be s' when the plural ends in s.
3. a PP will be 's when the plural does not end in s (changes form from the singular to the plural).
4. a real word must precede the apostrophe.

What is the PP of the word leaf? _____
What is the PP of the word family? _____

395

Using the 4 points given in the preceding frame as a guide, go back to Frame 391 and rework any that you missed the first time.

396

Punctuate these sentences with apostrophes:

A. *Girls clothing isnt as expensive as boys clothing. (several girls and boys)*
B. *Our companys policy hasnt been accepted too well by most workers in the plant. (one company)*

397

398

A. typists'   didn't   boss's
B. children's   mother's

399

Willis's tales
Willis' tales (Either is acceptable.)

400

C and D   (Phrase A: if the name is Gates, an apostrophe cannot come before the s.
Phrase B: there is only one Grand Canyon. Phrases C and D: when a name ends in s, ss, or x,
either an apostrophe (s') or an apostrophe s ('s) is appropriate.)

401

A. None
B. Marcus' (or Marcus's)   wasn't

402

A. town's
B. Ramona Richards' (or Richard's)   wasn't   judge's
C. None (Geneva Ross is the subject of the sentence.)

Punctuate the following:

    A. *The typists work didnt meet with the boss approval. (several typists, one boss)*
    B. *The childrens feelings were hurt by their mothers scolding words. (one mother)*

398

In making a person's name or a proper noun possessive, use an 's. Some authorities say that if the name ends in s, ss, or x, an apostrophe following the last letter is sufficient.

    Ex.: 1. James   =   James's   or James'
         2. Thoreaux =   Thoreaux's or Thoreaux'
         3. Bayless =   Bayless's   or Bayless'

What two ways using an apostrophe could you write this phrase?

    the tales of Willis

    _____

    _____

399

Again, a real word must precede the apostrophe.

    Ex.: Jones' or Jones's <u>not</u> <u>Jone's</u>

Circle the letter of the phrase that has the proper noun punctuated correctly:

    A. *Bud Gate's Electronics (Gates)*
    B. *The Grand Canyons' grandeur*
    C. *Raymond Landis's patience (Landis)*
    D. *Raymond Landis' patience (Landis)*

400

Pronouns, of course, do not require an apostrophe to show possession.

    Right: Yours, mine, and ours
    Wrong: The excuse is her's and their's

Put an apostrophe wherever necessary:

    A. *Yours was the only boat that was damaged.*
    B. *Marcus suggestion wasnt the same as theirs.*

401

Punctuate the following:

    A. *The towns main dump was located behind the house of Everett.*
    B. *Ramona Richards attorney wasnt one of the judges favorite lawyers. (Judge Jennifer Carter)*
    C. *Geneva Ross flew to Acapulco for two months.*

402

403

(A) (In Sentence B, *Secretary's* is a possessive word.)

404

It's impossible to understand all its meanings.

405

(B)

406

It's (It is the feeling of this committee that you be fined.)

407

it's

408

A. Your/s   Sammy Rogers' (or Rogers's)
B. Its selling feature is it/s ability. . .

409

A. Karen McWilliams' (or McWilliams's)   our/s   couldn't
B. Would/n't   our/s   Cy Hosler's?

Don't get carried away with the apostrophe. Be sure that the word possesses something before making it possessive.

Which sentence contains two plurals? (Circle the letter of the correct answer.)

    A. The girls asked their teachers to chaperone the senior prom.
    B. The Secretarys Handbook can answer most questions about letter style and format.

403

A common error is to confuse the pronoun *its* with the contraction *it's* (it is). Learn to distinguish between the two.

    Right: It's a grand night for singing. (It is a grand night. . .)
    Wrong: The tremendous social cost, however, is it's major drawback. (. . . however, is it is major drawback.)

Which is correct in parentheses? (Underline the correct answer.)

    (Its/It's) impossible to understand all (its/it's) meanings.

404

Which example below contains the pronoun *its*? (Circle the letter of the correct answer.)

    A. Its the feeling of this committee that you be fined.
    B. Did you see its bright colors?

405

Correct Sentence A in the preceding frame. _____

406

Anytime you aren't sure about whether to write *its* or *it's*, substitute the words *it is*. If you can use these words, you will want to write _____
                                                            (its/it's)

407

Insert and delete apostrophes as necessary in Frames 408 and 409:

    A. Your's is the only bicycle besides Sammy Roger's that I can ride. (Rogers)
    B. Its selling feature is it's ability to withstand heat.

408

    A. Karen McWilliams boat beat our's in the race, and it's too bad yours couldnt have finished. (McWilliams)
    B. Would'nt you even consider our's first before seeing Cy Hoslers? (Hosler)

409

410

Ⓔ

411

Ⓑ

412

Neither A nor B is correct. (Customer's in Sentence B)

413

Ⓑ

414

Frame 411:   manufacturers'
Frame 412:   one's   isn't   it's   you've
Frame 413:   Isabel's   isn't   it's

415

A. Can't you see Grant's mother, a 60-year-old lady, in a bikini?
B. Alex' (or Alex's) friend Rhonda, who is an artist in Pasadena's Rose Bowl Parade, won the president's trophy last year.

Which of the following sentences is correct? (Circle the letter of the correct answer.)

A. The Department of Labors Women's Bureau is concerned with the welfare of every industry's women.
B. The Department of Labors' Womens Bureau is concerned with the welfare of every industries women.
C. The Department of Labor's Women's Bureau is concerned with the welfare of every industries' women.
D. The Department of Labors Womens' Bureau is concerned with the welfare of every industry's women.
E. The Department of Labor's Women's Bureau is concerned with the welfare of every industry's women.
F. The Department of Labors Womens Bureau is concerned with the welfare of every industrys women.

410

Select the correct sentence in Frames 411, 412, and 413: (Circle the letter of the correct answer.)

A. Don't you see that the manufacturer's costs, as well as ours, are affected by style changes. (all manufacturers)
B. It's too bad you weren't able to hear the recital.

411

A. Borrowing on ones life insurance policy isnt recommended since its easy not to pay back the amount youve borrowed.
B. A customers opinion of a firm can be greatly influenced by the appearance of its employees.

412

A. Isabels advice was that auto insurance isnt a luxury; its a necessity.
B. A budget will not spend one's money, but it'll help one spend for those things wanted most.

413

Correct all of the errors in the A sentences in the last three frames:

Frame 411: _____

Frame 412: _____

Frame 413: _____

414

Punctuate this frame inserting any needed marks of punctuation: (Watch for other marks of punctuation inserted for review.)

A. Cant you see Grants mother a 60-year-old lady in a bikini
B. Alex friend Rhonda who is an artist in Pasadenas Rose Bowl Parade won the presidents trophy last year.

415

416

A. Let's   today;   can't   everyone's
B. It's   team's spirit; it's   don't

417

Parkins' (or Parkins's) week,   secretaries'

418

419

"Every individual endeavors to employ capital so that its produce may be of greatest value." (The period and comma are always placed inside the quotation marks.)

420

A. "boner"
B. "lulu." (Period inside the quotation marks)
NOTE: You should avoid using slang expressions in your own writing. Rather than apologize for the expression, avoid using it.
C. "eats up"

421

A. "recession"
B. "Macroeconomics"
C. "laissez-faire." (Period inside the quotation marks)

Punctuate the following:

A. *Lets try not to do too much today we cant solve everyones problems in a few hours.*
B. *Its not that I want to destroy the teams spirit its just that I dont see its usefulness anymore.*

416

Punctuate this sentence:

Parkins brother was here last week and he questioned the secretaries long coffee breaks.
(Parkins; many secretaries)

417

No response is required for this frame. Please read the material that follows.

The use of the quotation marks is rather infrequent in business; nevertheless, it might be well to know the following applications.

Use quotation marks to:

1. enclose the exact words of a speaker or a writer, or any quoted material.
2. set off slang expressions. (This tells the reader that you are aware the word is slang.)
3. set off unusual or technical words.
4. set off words intended to be emphasized.

418

Place quotation marks around the <u>quoted material</u> in the following sentence:

Adam Smith, political economist, stated the following: Every individual endeavors to employ capital so that its produce may be of greatest value.

419

What <u>slang</u> expressions below would you place in quotation marks?

A. *Wow! Did I ever pull a boner the other day!*
B. *The last quarter of yesterday's game was really a lulu.*
C. *Inflation literally eats up savings.*

420

Put quotation marks around the <u>technical</u> or <u>unusual</u> terms below:

A. *Economists use the word recession to mean a temporary falling off of business activity.*
B. *Macroeconomics is the study of the broad field of economics.*
C. *The word that commonly means to interfere very little is laissez-faire.*

421

422

    A. "mixed"
    B. "nervous system"

423

    A. "market."
    B. "rhubarb"
    C. "legal tender."
    D. "too much money chasing too few goods."
    NOTE: You may have chosen to punctuate differently. If so your way may be equally acceptable.

424

If you want to <u>emphasize</u> a word or a phrase, you may put quotes around it.

Ex.: Families should have an ''emergency fund'' of three to six times their monthly income.

Which words in the following sentences would you possibly want to emphasize?

422

A. *The U.S. government is a mixed economy in which both public and private institutions exercise economic control.*
B. *The office is frequently referred to as the nervous system of a business.*

Place quotation marks around the words below that:

1. are direct quotes.
2. are slang.
3. you wish to emphasize.
4. are technical terms.

423

A. *Decisions of what to produce, how much, and for whom are made through the market.*
B. *The dispute turned into a real rhubarb before the day was over.*
C. *Anything that is acceptable as money is called legal tender.*
D. *The popular version of inflation as stated by many economists is this: too much money chasing too few goods.*

Because the use of quotation marks is strictly at the option of the writer, you will not be required to use them either in the section test on the next page or on the final examination. If anything is meant to be in quotes, the quotation marks will be supplied.

424

Take Section Test 6. It emphasizes the use of the apostrophe and has a review of other punctuation. You do not need to worry about quotation marks.

February 12 19—

Mr Theodore Scott Sr
899 Borodin Drive
St Petersburg FL   33730-6281

Dear Mr Scott

Havent you often dreamed of owning your own beach cottage along Floridas Gulf Coast (E) Since you are probably like most people you may think your dreaming is mere fantasy (E) Well you arent dreaming I can assure you and Id like to take a few short paragraphs to tell you why (E)

Kreiger and Byers who are two of the best-known realtors in Florida have recently started a new housing development in Laurel a small community 15 miles south of Sarasota (E) Their latest predictions are that Laurels growth rate will quadruple by 1988 by June 1992 the citys population will be close to 30000 (thirty thousand) residents (E) The town which has no industry will continue to emphasize its reputation as a resort area (E) Therefore factories refineries chemical plants etc will all be banned and only residential units will be permitted to build within the city (E) This is not an affront to big business but it is an attempt to keep Laurel attractive and beautiful (E)

Ocean lots are currently priced at $8000 (eight thousand dollars) per half acre interior lots are as little as $4000 (four thousand dollars) per half acre (E) If you think you are ready to stop dreaming and turn a few of those dreams into reality come in and talk with Wes Kreiger or me (E) Well drive you down to the Gulf and you will see houses and proposed houses that you never dreamed could exist in Laurel (E)

    Wont you stop in at our convenient office soon and let us get
to know you personally (E) Were located on the corner of Welch and
Mulberry and you can be here in less than one hour from downtown St Pete
(E) Kreiger and Byers motto "dream and grow happy" is half fulfilled (E) You
have dreamed now it is time to grow happy (E)

                Very truly yours

                William Kerr

kk

February 12,[1]   19—

Mr?[2]   Theodore Scott,[3]   Sr.[4]
899 Borodin Drive
St.[5]   Petersburg,[6]   FL[7]   33730-6281[8]

Dear Mr.[9]   Scott:[10]

   Haven'[11]t you often dreamed of owning your own beach cottage along
Florida'[12]s Gulf Coast?[13]   Since you are probably like most people,[14]   you
may think your dreaming is mere fantasy.[15]   Well,[16] you aren'[17]t dreaming,[18]
I can assure you;[19]   and I'[20]d like to take a few short paragraphs to tell you
why?[21]

   Kreiger and Byers,[22] who are two of the best-known realtors in Florida,[23]
have recently started a new housing development in Laurel,[24] a small
community 15 miles south of Sarasota.[25] Their latest predictions are[26] that
Laurel'[27]s growth rate will quadruple by 1988;[28] by June[29]   1992[30] the
city'[31]s population will be close to 30,[32]000 residents.[33] The town,[34] which
has no industry,[35] will continue to emphasize its[36]   reputation as a resort
area.[37] Therefore,[38] factories,[39] refineries,[40] chemical plants,[41] etc.[42][43] will
all be banned;[44] and only residential units will be permitted to build within
the city.[45] This is not an affront to big business,[46] but it is an attempt to keep
Laurel attractive and beautiful.[47]

   Ocean lots are currently priced at $8,[48]000 per half acre;[49] interior lots
are as little as $4,[50]000 per half acre.[51] If you think you are ready to stop
dreaming[52] and turn a few of those dreams into reality,[53] come in[54] and talk
with Wes Kreiger or me.[55] We'[56]ll drive you down to the Gulf,[57] and you will
see houses and proposed houses that you never dreamed could exist in
Laurel.[58]

Won'[63]t you stop in at our convenient office soon[64] and let us get to know you personally.[65]   We'[66]re located on the corner of Welch and Mulberry,[67] and you can be here in less than one hour from downtown St.[68] Pete.[69] Kreiger and Byers'[70] motto,[71] "dream and grow happy,[72] " is half fulfilled.[73] You have dreamed;[74] now it is time to grow happy.[75]

Very truly yours,[76]

William Kerr

kk

SECTION 6
REVIEW SHEET

If you missed no.	See Frame no.	If you missed no.	See Frame no.	If you missed no.	See Frame no.
1	101	26	274	51	2 & 4
2	15	27	380 & 399	52	313 & 316
3	125	28	342 & 348	53	157 & 162
4	15	29	92	54	313 & 316
5	15	30	92	55	2 & 4
6	103	31	380 & 399	56	375 & 376
7	107	32	49 & 50	57	307 & 311
8	53	33	2 & 4	58	2 & 4
9	15	34	275 & 283	59	15
10	138 & 149	35	277 & 283	60	125
11	375 & 376	36	404 & 407	61	15
12	380 & 399	37	2 & 4	62	101
13	10	38	226 & 228	63	375 & 376
14	157 & 162	39	57 & 58	64	313 & 316
15	2 & 4	40	57 & 58	65	32 & 33
16	215	41	73	66	375 & 376
17	375 & 376	42	15	67	307 & 311
18	201 & 203	43	73	68	15
19	329 & 330	44	329 & 330	69	2 & 4
20	375 & 376	45	2 & 4	70	380 & 399
21	2 & 4	46	307	71	245 & 255
22	277 & 285	47	2 & 4	72	245
23	277 & 283	48	49 & 50	73	2 & 4
24	245 & 266	49	342 & 348	74	342 & 348
25	2 & 4	50	49 & 50	75	2 & 4
				76	136 & 149

Please turn to page 213 to record Section 6 test errors and to restudy any particular rules with which you are still having difficulty.

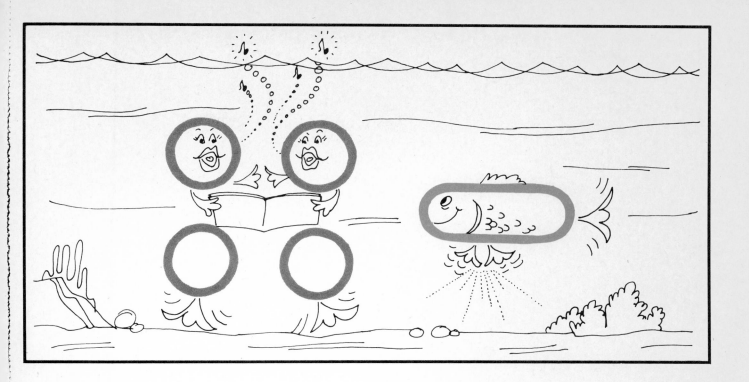

Learning is not rote memorization—it is being able to apply what you know.

SECTION 7

Application Summary

. . . **Colon** in expressing time
. . . **Colon** in introducing a list, an explanation, or a formal quotation
. . . **Hyphen** between a compound adjective preceding the noun

425

7:45 a.m.

426

A. 8:05
B. 11:30 to 12:15

427

Ⓑ (Time may be expressed with or without the a.m. or p.m. Never does a space precede or follow the colon in expressing time.)

428

7 p.m. or 7:00 p.m. (Notice that no colon is used when the time is stated without the zeroes—NOT 10: p.m. or 7: p.m.

429

as follows
The following

430

sources:

As a routine mark of punctuation, a colon is used to separate hours and minutes in expressing time.

Ex.: 9:30 a.m.   6:15 p.m.

Use a colon in the following phrase:

She arrived at 7 45 a.m.

425

Write the hours and minutes correctly in these sentences:

A. *Continental's flight leaves at _____ (five after eight).*
B. *My lunch hour is from _____ (eleven thirty) to _____ (twelve fifteen).*

426

Which is correct? (Circle the letter of the correct answer.)

A. *Wanda left at 6-52 p.m.*
B. *The 8:12 train from Cleveland is late.*
C. *You asked about the 10: 15 session.*

427

Frequently, on-the-hour times are stated with <u>no</u> colon or zeroes.

Ex.: Our appointment is for 10 a.m.

In the above example either 10 a.m. or 10:00 a.m. would be considered correct.

Write seven o'clock p.m. two ways using figures: _____ _____

428

The colon is also used to introduce a list, an explanation, examples, or a formal quotation. An expression such as *the following* or *as follows* commonly precedes the list.

Ex.: 1. The list of supplies needed is as follows: bond paper, letterhead envelopes, paper clips, carbon paper, and ink.
2. The following description best defines a budget: an estimate of expected income and a plan for expenditures.

In the first example the enumeration is introduced by the words _____ _____.
In the second example the words _____ _____ introduce the enumeration.

429

Where would you place a colon in this sentence?

Uncle Sam's money comes from the following three sources individual income taxes, corporate income taxes, and employment taxes.

430

431

No.

432

(A)   (By using a colon in Sentence B, you are separating the verb from the predicate complement.)

433

Yes.

434

No. A complete sentence does not precede the colon.

435

United Airlines has two nonstop flights to Dallas: one at 10:15 and another at 12:30.

436

(B)

One thing to remember about using a colon in an enumeration is that a complete sentence must <u>precede</u> the colon.

Ex.: The functions of banks are these: holding, transferring, and lending money.

Does a complete sentence come before the colon in these sentences? _____
(Yes/No)

A. *Some of the services banks offer are: checking account service, savings account service, and lending money.*
B. *One of the best reasons for buying on credit is: to prove that you pay your bills promptly.*

431

In which example does a complete sentence precede the colon? (Circle the letter of the correct answer.)

A. *There is one thing you should remember about spending: The real cost of any particular item is equal to all the things you can no longer buy.*
B. *The various types of banks are: commercial, mutual, industrial, and savings and loan.*

432

To complete the sentence before the colon in Sentence B of the preceding frame, you could write the following:

1. The various types of banks are <u>these</u>: commercial, mutual, industrial, and savings and loan.
2. <u>These</u> are the various types of banks: commercial, mutual, industrial, and savings and loan.
3. The various types of banks are <u>as follows</u>: commercial, mutual, industrial, and savings and loan.

Does a complete sentence now precede the colon in the rewritten examples above? _____ (Yes/No)

433

A colon throws the emphasis forward to the material following it and may be used only after a complete sentence.

Fringe benefits include: paid sick leave, pensions, insurance, and hospitalization programs.

Is the sentence above correct? _____ Why? _____
(Yes/No)

434

Punctuate this sentence:

United Airlines has two nonstop flights to Dallas one at 10 15 and another at 12 30.

435

In which of the examples below is the colon used correctly? (Circle the letter of the correct answer.)

A. *The subjects I'm taking this semester are: history, economics, typing, English, and chemistry.*
B. *I am taking the following subjects this semester: history, economics, typing, English, and chemistry.*

436

437

Ⓐ

438

Ⓑ

439

The two principal goals of insurance are these: . . .
These are the two principal goals of insurance: . . .
The following are the two principal goals of insurance: . . .
The two principal goals of insurance are as follows: . . .
There are two principal goals of insurance: . . .
(Can you think of any more ways to write it?)

440

A. If

441

A. The sentence is correct.
B. Goods and services are those things which have . . .

442

A. as follows: Individuals shouldn't
B. No colon after are. proprietorship, the partnership, and the corporation. (a series)

Which sentence is correct in Frames 437 and 438? (Circle the letter of the correct answer.)

437

A. *A large increase in the total supply of money would have this result: It would cause an increase in prices.*

B. *A large increase in the total supply of money would result in: an increase in prices.*

438

A. *The most important feature of insurance is: its ability to provide for unexpected and very large casualty.*

B. *The most important feature of insurance is this: its ability to provide for unexpected and very large casualty.*

The colon used in the sentence below is wrong. Rewrite the sentence so that the colon is correct:

439

The two principal goals of insurance are: to provide for the family and to build a reserve of funds.

_____

_____

You know that a complete sentence must precede the colon. Sometimes a complete sentence will also <u>follow</u> the colon. In this case the first word after the colon should be capitalized.

440

Which word in the sentences below should be capitalized after the colon? _____

A. *Remember this: <u>if</u> savers hoarded their money rather than invested it, business couldn't expand.*

B. *The definition of capitalism is this: <u>the</u> voluntary accumulation of capital through savings by individuals to finance production.*

Insert and delete punctuation as necessary:

441

A. *Capital consists of the following: buildings, machines, and other durable goods.*

B. *Goods and services are: those things which have usefulness in satisfying human wants.*

Punctuate the following sentences:

442

A. *A rule of thumb for buying a home is as follows individuals shouldnt pay more than 2½ times their annual income for a house.*

B. *The three most important types of business organizations today are the sole proprietorship the partnership and the corporation.*

443

Corporate bonds are considered a safer investment than stocks for this reason: If a corporation fails, bondholders are creditors; that is, they must be paid before stockholders.

444

seven-story building

445

(A)   (Do you see that rock-bottom is read as one modifier? Beautiful and floor both modify sample, but they modify it separately.)

446

No.

447

A. ever-changing society
B. None
C. error-free manuscript

448

adjectives
adverbs

449

(B)   (A face-to-face confrontation)

Punctuate this review sentence:

Corporate bonds are considered a safer investment than stocks for this reason if a corporation fails bondholders are creditors that is they must be paid before stockholders.

443

Use a hyphen when two or more words have the force of a single modifier before a noun. Such words are called *compound adjectives*.

Ex.: 1. high-priced merchandise
2. an up-to-date report

Punctuate the following sentence:

The <u>seven</u> <u>story</u> building was demolished.

444

Two adjectives often precede the noun they modify. If the two adjectives are meant to be read as one, a hyphen should be inserted between them.

Which adjectives below should be read as <u>one</u> modifier? (Circle the letter of the correct answer.)

A. We are selling at <u>rock bottom</u> prices.
B. This model is a <u>beautiful floor</u> sample.

445

Are these adjectives compound (to be read as one)? _____

(Yes/No)

A. a giant clearance sale
B. a big black bear

446

Punctuate the two compound adjectives below:

A. our ever changing society
B. an excellent tennis coach
C. an error free manuscript

447

Adverbs, which usually end in <u>ly</u>, are not compounded with adjectives. Therefore, no hyphen should be used between an adverb and an adjective before a noun.

Ex.: 1. high-priced merchandise   <u>but</u>   high<u>ly</u> priced merchandise
2. a slow-moving car   <u>but</u>   a slow<u>ly</u> moving car

In the above examples high and slow are _____; highly and slowly are _____.

448

Which of these phrases needs a hyphen? (Circle the letter of the correct answer.)

A. a professionally drawn painting
B. a face to face confrontation

449

450

Ⓐ

451

Ⓐ   (Numbers used as adjectives when compounded with other words are <u>always</u> hyphenated.)

452

Ⓑ

453

Neither is correct. (The two adjectives in both instances modify the noun separately.)

454

Ⓐ   (Follow up in Sentence B is used as an infinitive, not as an adjective.)

455

A. heart-warming (*Sharply* is an adverb.)
B. awe-inspiring
C. foreign-made (*Newly* is an adverb.)

456

A. well-dressed business person
B. well-deserved reputation

457

Ⓐ   (*Well* is used as a noun, not an adjective, in Sentence B.)

Which phrase in Frames 450 and 451 needs a hyphen? (Circle the letter of the correct answer.)

    A. *a long term plan*
    B. *a badly executed play*

450

    A. *a three hour meeting*
    B. *the privately owned yacht*

451

Once again, before hyphenating be sure the adjectives are meant to be read together as one unit. Which phrase is correct in Frames 452, 453, and 454? (Circle the letter of the correct answer.)

    A. *an old-grizzly bear*
    B. *a year-end sale*

452

    A. *a worthless-baby carriage*
    B. *the talented-personnel manager*

453

    A. *send a follow-up letter*
    B. *He wanted to follow-up the letter*

454

Hyphenate between the compound adjectives:

    A. *The sharply dressed entertainer sang a heart warming medley.*
    B. *Our minister gave an awe inspiring sermon last Sunday.*
    C. *The newly decorated living room was done in foreign made objects.*

455

Most words compounded with *well* are hyphenated when the adjectives <u>precede</u> the nouns they modify.

    Ex.: 1. a well-read person
         2. our well-educated people

Punctuate the following:

    A. *a well dressed business person*
    B. *the well deserved reputation*

456

Which phrase would need a hyphen? (Circle the letter of the correct answer.)

    A. *your well rounded personality*
    B. *a large oil well was found*

457

458

follows   no hyphen
precedes   a hyphen

459

460

serious looking ___√___

461

A. None
B. None
C. 40-minute lecture. (Numbers are always hyphenated when they appear with another adjective before a noun.)

462

No. __3__
No. __2__
No. __1__
No. __4__

463

A. (The compound adjective precedes the noun.)
B. (The compound adjective follows the noun *punishment*.)
C. (*Correctly* is an adverb.)
D. (*Party-loving* is a compound adjective before the noun it modifies.)
E. (The adjectives *high* and *brick* modify fence separately.)

Now that you have the compound adjective *well* in mind, remember this very important modification: If the compound adjective follows the noun it modifies, no hyphen will be necessary.

    Right: The up-to-date office
    Right: Our office is kept up to date

As shown above if the compound adjective (precedes/follows) the noun it modifies, (a hyphen/no hyphen) is required.

458

In which sentence does the compound adjective follow the noun? (Circle the letter of the correct answer.)

    A. *Our furniture is low priced.*
    B. *He is a serious looking individual.*

459

Which compound adjective in the preceding frame would need a hyphen? (Check the correct answer.)

    low priced   _____
    serious looking   _____

460

Hyphenate the following wherever needed:

    A. *The child was well mannered.*
    B. *The candy was sold house to house.*
    C. *The professor gave a 40 minute lecture.*

461

You know that:

    1. compound adjectives preceding the noun <u>are</u> hyphenated.
    2. compound adjectives following the noun <u>are not</u> hyphenated.
    3. two separate adjectives <u>are not</u> hyphenated.
    4. adverbs (ly) and adjectives <u>are not</u> hyphenated.

Which rules above apply to these phrases?

    the Grand Ole Opry   No. _____
    Kelly's good fortune was well deserved   No. _____
    a long-distance telephone call   No. _____
    a suddenly appearing storm   No. _____

462

Circle the letters of the sentences that are correct:

    A. *I received a first-class package today.*
    B. *Jackie's punishment was well-deserved.*
    C. *A correctly-stated rule will be clear.*
    D. *Three party-loving persons lived right beside us.*
    E. *The driver hit a high-brick fence.*

463

464

465

A. self-destructive
B. self-inflicted

466

A. self-discipline
B. None
C. Correct as is

467

The word is not hyphenated because it is <u>over</u> one hundred. (125 would be written one hundred twenty-five.)

468

A. not-too-distant future
B. well-purchased home (The first compound adjective precedes the noun; the second follows the noun.)

469

All three are correct.
(A.) (*White-collar* is a compound adjective preceding the noun *jobs*.)
(B.) (*Never-ending* is a compound adjective preceding the noun *process*.)
(C.) (*Well aware* <u>follows</u> the pronoun *we*; *poorly* is an adverb.)

470

A. goods-producing society . . .
B. the following: <u>F</u>armers will use long-term credit . . .

No response is required for this frame. Please read the following:

> *Some words such as* brother-in-law, window-shopping, letter-perfect, get-together, *and* double-park *are always hyphenated. There are no rules to follow. The best advice is to consult a good dictionary.*

464

You can be certain that most *self* words will be hyphenated no matter if they precede or follow the noun. (The few exceptions are *selfish*, *selfhood*, *selfless*, and *selfsame*.)

Punctuate the following:

A. *Some people are self destructive.*
B. *Lou's wounds were self inflicted.*

465

Punctuate these sentences:

A. *Most people could stand a little more self discipline.*
B. *Don't be so selfish.*
C. *We sent a self-explanatory brochure.*

466

Compound numbers <u>under</u> one hundred are always hyphenated when they are written out.

Right: We paid ninety-three dollars.
Wrong: The old man was eighty six.

Why is this word not hyphenated? _____

One hundred twenty

467

Insert and delete hyphens as necessary:

A. *Within the not too distant future, more and more Americans will live in less-crowded rural areas.*
B. *A well purchased home is still a good investment if it is well financed.*

468

Which sentence below is correct? (Circle the letter of the correct answer.)

A. *The number of people employed in white-collar jobs is increasing.*
B. *Education should be thought of as a never-ending process.*
C. *We were well aware of the poorly lighted office.*

469

Punctuate the following sentences:

A. *We have shifted from a goods producing society to one that is service producing.*
B. *In the future we can expect the following farmers will use long term credit for purchasing highly expensive equipment.*

470

471

A. one fact: The fast-moving American economy
B. on-the-spot coverage.

472

473

A. Well/over   Middle/East
B. easily/read headlines, and/ miscellaneous business-related information/

474

No.

475

These numbers were the winning numbers in New Jersey's lottery: thirty-two, twenty-eight, ninety-seven, and forty-three.

Punctuate the following sentences:

A. *Everyone knows this one fact The fast moving American economy is consumer oriented.*
B. *CBS News is noted for its on the spot coverage.*

471

Circle the letter of the sentence that is correct:

A. *The connecting flight, which departs at 4:30 p.m., will require a two-hour delay.*
B. *The connecting flight, which departs at 4:30 pm, will require a two hour delay.*

472

Delete punctuation marks that are not needed in the sentences below:

A. *Well-over one-third of all our oil is imported from the Middle-East.*
B. *You can receive up-to-the-minute stock quotations, live sports coverage, easily-read headlines, and, miscellaneous business-related information, from cable television.*

473

Is this sentence correct? _____
(Yes/No)

These numbers were the winning numbers in New Jersey's lottery, thirty two, twenty eight, ninety seven and forty three.

474

Punctuate the preceding sentence as it should be punctuated.

_____
_____

475

C O N G R A T U L A T I O N S ! ! !

You have just completed the entire program. Take the section test that follows and then consult the instructor regarding the instructions for taking the final examination. This exam should be completed immediately.

SECTION 7 TEST

December 26 19—

Coppes Nappanee Kitchens Inc
Attention Mr I M Bradley Jr
500 East Market Street
Nappanee IN   46550-1111

Ladies and Gentlemen

On June 13 1982 my husband and I will be moving into a new home (E) My husband who was born and raised in Wakarusa Indiana claims that Nappanee kitchens without a doubt are among the best in the world (E) Therefore Im writing to ask if we can make an appointment for Thursday January 25 at 11 30 a m to come to your factory to see some of your ready built displays (E) After being away for 12 years we are planning to visit Nappanee to mix pleasure and business (E)

Since we will be landing at the local airport would you mind asking Frances Wilson one of my husbands high school friends to meet us (E) Mrs Wilson president of Nappanee Kitchens has been awaiting this long overdue visit for years and I am certain shell be looking forward to seeing us (E) Our schedule will be as follows

Thurs	8 45	Arrive at the airport
	9 30	Check in at the 50 room Hollander Hotel
	11 30	Visit Robert Coppes showroom
	4 00	Attend the 15 year class reunion
Fri	10 45	Board the plane for Atlanta

If you have a kitchen which we really like well purchase it the same day as our visit (E) These are the prime features we are looking for in our all electric kitchen an eye level oven a built in microwave oven a double porcelain sink a built in dishwasher and rosewood cabinets (E) The total cost of such a "dream" kitchen we hope will be less than $9500 (nine thousand, five hundred dollars) (E)

203

We look forward to our trip to Nappanee and we hope that you are able to supply us with a kitchen that is low priced but high in quality (E) It will be great seeing everyone and being home again (E)

Cordially yours

Mrs B Barnett

am

December 26,[1] 19—[2]

Coppes'[3] Nappanee Kitchens,[4] Inc.[5]
Attention Mr.[6] I[7] M.[8] Bradley,[9] Jr.[10]
500 East Market Street
Nappanee,[11] IN[12]   46550-1111[13]

Ladies and Gentlemen:[14]

On June 13,[15] 1982,[16] my husband and I will be moving into a new home.[17] My husband,[18] who was born and raised in Wakarusa,[19] Indiana,[20] claims that Nappanee kitchens,[21] without a doubt,[22] are among the best in the world.[23] Therefore,[24] I'm[25] writing to ask if we can make an appointment for Thursday,[26] January 25,[27] at 11:[28]30 a.[29]m. to come to your factory to see some of your ready[30]built displays.[31] After being away for 12 years,[32] we are planning to visit Nappanee to mix pleasure and business.[33]

Since we will be landing at the local airport,[34] would you mind asking Frances Wilson,[35] one of my husband'[36]s high school friends,[37] to meet us[38]* Mrs.[39] Wilson,[40] president of Nappanee Kitchens,[41] has been awaiting this long[42]overdue visit for years;[43] and I am certain she'll[44] be looking forward to seeing us.[45] Our schedule will be as follows:[46]

Thurs.[47]	8:45 [48]	Arrive at the airport
	9:30	Check in at the 50[49]room Hollander Hotel
	11:30	Visit Robert Coppes'[50] showroom
	4:00	Attend the 15[51]year class reunion
Fri.	10:45	Board the plane for Atlanta

If you have a kitchen[53] which we really like,[54] we'll[55] purchase it the same day as our visit.[56] These are the prime features we are looking for in our all[57]electric kitchen:[58] an eye[59]level oven,[60] a built[61]in microwave oven,[62] a double[63] procelain sink,[64] a built[65]in dishwasher[66]* and rosewood cabinets[67] The total cost of such a "dream" kitchen,[68] we hope,[69] will be less than $9,[70]500.[71]

Coppes'[72] Nappanee Kitchens[73] Inc[74]   -2-   December 26[75] 19—

    We look forward to our trip to Nappanee[76] and we hope that you are able to supply us with a kitchen that is low priced[77] but high in quality[78] It will be great seeing everyone[79] and being home again[80]

                    Cordially yours[81]

                    Mrs[82] B[83] Barnett

am

(The * indicates that the punctuation is optional.)

SECTION 7
REVIEW SHEET

If you missed no.	See Frame no.	If you missed no.	See Frame no.	If you missed no.	See Frame no.
1	101	29	15	57	444 & 445
2	101	30	444 & 445	58	429 & 434
3	380 & 399	31	2 & 4	59	444 & 445
4	129	32	157 & 162	60	57 & 60
5	15	33	2 & 4	61	444 & 445
6	15	34	157 & 162	62	57 & 60
7	15	35	245 & 266	63	452
8	15	36	380 & 399	64	57 & 60
9	125	37	245 & 253	65	444 & 445
10	15	38	10	66	57 & 59
11	103	39	15	67	2 & 4
12	107	40	119	68	201 & 203
13	53	41	119	69	201 & 204
14	138 & 149	42	444 & 445	70	49 & 50
15	90 & 97	43	329 & 330	71	2 & 4
16	90 & 97	44	375 & 376	72	380 & 399
17	2 & 4	45	2 & 4	73	129
18	275 & 276	46	429 & 434	74	15
19	103	47	15	75	101
20	103 & 275	48	425	76	307
21	201 & 203	49	444 & 451	77	313
22	201 & 204	50	380 & 399	78	2 & 4
23	2 & 4	51	444 & 451	79	313
24	226 & 228	52	15	80	2 & 4
25	375 & 376	53	275 & 283	81	136 & 149
26	91 & 97	54	157 & 162	82	15
27	97	55	375 & 376	83	15
28	425	56	2 & 4		

Please turn to page 214 to record Section 7 test errors and restudy any punctuation rules with which you are still having difficulty.

SECTION 1

Directions: On the following blank pages (one page for each of the seven sections of this text), you are to record the punctuation rules that are still giving you trouble. This first sheet is for recording any errors made on the Section 1 test.

For every punctuation error made, write an example phrase or a sentence using the punctuation mark in proper context. Do not copy any material given in this text—you are to write your own examples. If you are uncertain, or cannot understand the rule after carefully re-studying it, ask your instructor to assist you.

This process is very important. You should not continue in the program until you understand not only <u>why</u> you made specific errors but also <u>how</u> to correct those errors in your writing. When you can begin to employ your new-found skill in your work, you will make even greater strides toward punctuation proficiency.

SECTION 2

SECTION 3

SECTION 4

SECTION 5

SECTION 6

SECTION 7